May
God
Bless!

Tim
& Cheryl

Blinded, But Now I See

"It's Not Just about Me"

Written by Jane E. Morin

Library of Congress Control Number: 2013913839

Printed in the United States of America.

This book is printed on acid-free paper.

Scriptures taken from the Holy Bible, New International Version®, NIV®. Copyright © 1973, 1978, 1984, 2011 by Biblica, Inc.™ Used by permission of Zondervan. All rights reserved worldwide. www.zondervan.com The "NIV" and "New International Version" are trademarks registered in the United States Patent and Trademark Office by Biblica, Inc.™ All rights reserved.

Any people depicted in stock imagery provided by Thinkstock are models, and such images are being used for illustrative purposes only. Certain stock imagery © Thinkstock.

Dedicated to the loving memory
of Tony Crow's parents,
R.D. "Cotton" Crow and Pearlie Jo "Hill" Crow

Isaiah 42:16

"I will lead the blind by ways they have not known, along unfamiliar paths, I will guide them; I will turn the darkness into light before them and make the rough places smooth. These are the things that I will do; I will not forsake them."

(NIV) New International Version

TABLE OF CONTENTS

FOREWORD

Tony Crow or simply "Crow"—is my friend and is the prime example of "what you see is what you get." He is one of the least pretentious men I have ever met and is genuinely comfortable in his own skin—which is usually covered in blue jeans, a shirt, boots, a cap, and his trademark sunglasses.

Crow and I have come to be great friends over the years. We have bonded over faith, family, dominoes, cows, and hunting. We have enjoyed many adventures and good times in spite of living very separate lives for the past several years. Every time we get together, it's like my family and I had never left Winnsboro, meaning that we seemed to pick up conversations at the exact spot we left off. (If you are around Crow much, you will know that he is always talking, which is great since that's how he makes his living these days.)

I have pleasant memories with Crow, but I will

never forget the night that we received the phone call about his accident. My wife and I got to the hospital in Dallas shortly after he arrived. The heart aches of that night will not ever be forgotten, nor the image of his face in the ER as I was asked to come see him before his surgeries.

Those who thought that Crow would slow down after his accident clearly did not know Tony Crow. He rebounded from his accident with purpose and a drive to continue to live his life to the fullest in spite of being blind. I am continually amazed at some of the things he continues to do or relearns to do in spite of his handicap. His determination and perseverance to overcome are inspirational to all of us fortunate enough to call him a friend.

Crow is my 42 partner. For those not familiar with the game, it is a domino game similar to the card game spades, and yes, we still play 42 in spite of the fact that he cannot see the dominoes. We have played as partners countless times, over 25 years usually against our arch nemesis, Donnie Stone and Billy Edwards. We have won a lot and lost a few times. In a way, the game represents life as every hand is a new game. Tony and his wife Cheryl took an absolutely awful loss, and turned it into a life that impacts and serves people.

I thank God for friends like Tony and Cheryl Crow, and I believe that you will be inspired and motivated as you read his story.

May God bless you as you enjoy this book.

Joe Ward

Executive Pastor

Georgetown, Texas—First Baptist Church

FROM TONY CROW

I want to first of all thank my loving wife who has stood beside me during this most difficult and life-changing event. Without Cheryl's total support and encouragement, I don't think I would be where I am today. Candace, our amazing and loving daughter, you have always been an inspiration to me as you give of yourself and to others. Your genuine loving and caring attitude touches so many lives that you come in contact with. Thank you for always being an example of God's love and for continually praying for me. You will always be Daddy's little girl. Landon—Son, you are my best friend, and I am so proud of the man you have become. You have always been a hard worker with a tender heart. You are a rock that I lean on, and I look forward to hearing from you nearly every day as you share with me about your hunts and your daily activities. So many times people ask how this accident has affected our relationship: it has only made the bond tighter. Our beautiful Julie, we are so thankful for the love that you have for Landon. We are proud to call you family. Our precious, beautiful granddaughter Macy—I look forward to many years of being the best blind "Pepa" that I can be to you.

To the community of Winnsboro, our friends, and our FBC church family, I thank you for the continued support that you surrounded us with when this life-changing accident occurred. It turned our world upside down, but so many of you were there to support my family and me. I am proud to call Winnsboro, Texas, my home.

To my friends and co-workers at Texas Utilities (now called Luminant Energy), I am so thankful for my years of work with such a great group of people. We have raised our families together as we talked daily about them. Thank you all for the unbelievable support that you gave to my family and me. Today, I am still in contact with so many of you, and that is something for which I will always be thankful. I enjoy each opportunity I have to come back to the plant to visit with all of you.

To all my new friends that I have had the opportunity to meet at safety presentations all over the world, I hope that something that you have heard in my presentation or read in this book will stay with you the rest of your life. I hope that you understand the importance of safety 24/7 at work, at home, and in play. Accidents change lives forever. My hope and prayer is that you will take safety to a new level and make it a personal goal to always watch out for yourself and those around you.

Last but not least, I thank my Lord and Savior, Jesus Christ, for dying on the cross for my sins because one day I will see again.

May God bless you and your family.

Tony Crow

PREFACE

When friends and peers began to tell me to put my life story into a book, I literally laughed out loud. I could not imagine someone like myself having anything to offer to others that would be earth shaking or revolutionary. As a public speaker standing in front of thousands of people regularly, I never once dreamed that I would be where I am today. However, encouraged by my friends and family, I decided to share the event that changed my life and theirs forever. One day I was out hunting with my son, and the next moment the world became entirely black. Since that day, there has been no change.

My hope is that once you read my life-changing story that you will understand that the choices we make now, affect our lives later. That ignoring well-known safety practices can leave you forever changed and affect not only you, but your family and friends. This book is not just about me—it is about you, about mankind and about those we love the most.

I want to thank Jane Morin, the author of this book for her ability to put into words what is in my heart and what I want my readers to understand. Don't feel sorry for me. God has taken me to a new place where I see better now than I ever have before. Come along with me on this journey, and I can promise you two things: first—that you will never think of safety in the same way you do right now, and second, that we most certainly will share a smile or two.

Jane Morin, is an award-winning author and radio host. Morin has been ghostwriting books and other literary material for over twenty years. She has authored several award-winning projects, including her own, *"Forty Days of Life-Changing Devotions"* and her most recent release *"21 Days of Renewal and Spiritual Awakening: Unveiling the Bride of Christ."* Morin is not only a successful ghostwriter, but she travels internationally speaking at conferences and leading worship events as well as serving as the Director of Missions for her own ministry. Morin currently resides with her husband in West Texas.

When Tony Crow's wife, Cheryl, met Morin on a trip to Israel, and realized that she was a successful writer, she asked Morin to consider writing Tony's story.

After multiple interviews with Tony Crow's friends, peers, co-workers and family members, Morin felt that she had gained the knowledge to write his biography. She spent several days at the farm observing how Tony and Cheryl were coping with his loss of eyesight, and how the community of Winnsboro has rallied around them to support their efforts. She saw that out of such tragedy came new vision and purpose as Tony Crow now travels the country telling others of his life-changing story.

Although Crow gladly cooperated with the project, he wanted the project to be written from the voice and perspective of the author, Jane Morin. With very few limitations placed on the project, Morin was able to capture the essence of the Crow family and their values. Throughout this project, you will find lessons of leadership, honesty and integrity that make Tony Crow the person he is today.

PREFACE

In the winter of 2011, I was on a ministry trip in Israel, when I met Cheryl Crow, the illustrious wife of Tony Crow. No, she is not the famous star known as Sheryl Crow, nor does she sign autographs as some people may actually believe. However, Tony Crow, without a doubt, would say she is his star and confidant in everything that takes place regarding their lives at home and on the road as he travels to speak nationwide. The first thing I noticed about Cheryl was her beautiful salt and pepper hair, her curls that fell just above her shoulders, and her piercing blue eyes coupled with her genuine smile that quickly put me at ease. I actually got to know her daughter Candace on the trip slightly more, as I dutifully summoned her as my ministry photographer while traveling, after seeing her gift behind the lens. After meeting Cheryl, she asked me about my writing career, and I suggested that when she got home to contact me about writing the life story of Tony Crow. So, here we are.

Before I did field work on this project, Cheryl sent me a DVD of the presentation that Tony does nationwide. Once I watched it, I knew then that this was no ordinary project. It did not take long for me to be captivated and intrigued by this family. I am honored to be the one given the opportunity to write their story. I know that Tony is a savvy guy when it comes to business, and though he had many opportunities to become a foreman at his previous job, he always declined. He did not want that kind of responsibility, and when I think about it, I can understand why. His job already gave him enough responsibility as he worked in the control room for a large electric company. The decisions he made daily on the job could put others at risks if not acted upon wisely and with a sound mind. Adding more responsibility to his existing job would seem overwhelming to most people, though all of Tony's co-workers believed he could handle it. He just was not ready at the time to *prove* that he could.

A few months after arriving home from Israel, I flew into Dallas, TX, rented a car and started out to meet with the Crow family. Before I left for Winnsboro, I met up with Candace Crow, their daughter, in Dallas. I was able to interview her to gain her perspective before heading out to Crow Angus Farms.

After arriving at Crow Angus Farms, I was quickly introduced to Tony Crow, who was sitting outside at the glass patio table surrounded with four wicker chairs. He had his trusted guide dog Rudy by his side. Tony is about six feet tall with fair, freckled skin that is slightly weathered by the east Texas sun. At fifty-five years of age, he has thinning, curly white hair and a white mustache to match. When I met him that day, he was wearing blue work overalls and a baseball hat. As a broad smile appeared across his face, he stood and held his hand out to greet me.

One thing you will find out about Tony is that he possesses a contagious smile that causes the rest of the world to smile with him. It does not matter what kind of tragic event he has experienced in the past, or the kind of rough day he might be experiencing now, Tony's upbeat personality, helps him keep things in the right perspective. Many times, I found myself in awe of his response to this life-shattering change that made him the man he is today. My prayer is that you will see a life that is determined, self-dependent, and strong-willed become molded in the Master's hand. You will find that as a result of tragedy, genuine compassion has woven its way into Tony Crow's heart like never before. One thing is for sure, Tony Crow is a *man on a mission, with a message* that changes lives, and *a* monumental passion to make sure that no one who crosses his path will make the same mistake that he did.

CHAPTER ONE

Where It All Began

After visiting the historic township of Winnsboro, I can fathom why Tony says it is a privilege to have lived here all of his life. Driving through the rolling hills of Winnsboro, Texas one can easily experience the sensation of having stepped back into a time when life was a bit simpler, and when folks genuinely cared for one another. Winnsboro is located 90 miles east of Dallas, TX: naturally, much like any other small town of approximately 3500 people, it remains a community where everyone tends to know everyone else. Originally known as The Crossroads, Winnsboro began to make a name for itself in the early 1850's. Though the sense of community has existed here since its founding, there is a driving force behind this picturesque farm town that keeps it thriving. Once you meet the folks you begin to comprehend what that force is. If you take a drive down the long, winding road of farmlands and meadows surrounded by pastures of cattle and the irrepressible scent of spring permeating the air, you will soon arrive at Crow Angus Farms. The one hundred and twenty-five acres nestled in the middle of east Texas is breathtaking and beckons one to moments of solitude and retreat. To both Tony and Cheryl, this four-generation homestead is simply called, "home." It does not take anyone a long time to figure out why Tony's family has held on to this prominent place in Winnsboro. When you drive up to the addition that they built in the early eighties you catch on right away that though their ranch home is filled with beautiful antiques and decorated with all the comforts of a classic country home, that they are much like everyone else here, down to earth, approachable and that they possess something that many homes in America are lacking, a sense of both pride and humility.

Tony Gale Crow was born in Mount Pleasant, TX on Sept 24, 1956. As the youngest son of Robert Deary Crow and Pearlie Jo (Hill) Crow, he always counted it a privilege to be a part of such an incredible heritage. Tony's earliest memory as a child was at the age of two. "*I had a hernia operation, and I suppose the drama of that and the pain incurred, seared that memory into my conscious. Nevertheless, I have been gifted with an uncanny knack for remembering specific details, and I suppose as I am remembering fundamental elements for this book that my memory has been key to my success today.*"

Tony will say without hesitation that the most influential person in his life was his father. "*I idolized my Daddy. He was everything to me! I wanted to be just like him when I grew up. Even as an adult, I looked up to him and respected him as he was always a great example of a man to emulate.*"

As I was sitting out on the patio with Tony and questioning him about his life, the accident, and his family, initially it caused some apprehension on his part in regard to following through with the project.

Concerned that the book would become boastful of his accomplishments or sensationalize the tragedy that brought him to where he is today, he expressed his uneasiness at the matter. It was distinctly clear to me that Tony, unlike most public speakers, is uncomfortable talking about himself. As charming as that sounds, I imagined it to be the reason why many respected folks in the community, and the grove of friends he has established through the years, genuinely care about him and would do anything for him. I know this, not because they said so, but merely because I can see what Tony cannot realize when he is interacting with his friends. There is genuine admiration and love reflected in their faces as they converse or cut up with him. Like many of his friends, Tony has an incredible sense of humor. For instance, at a simple gathering to partake of the supper meal, the evening was filled with nonstop laughter, jokes and the ordinary camaraderie that develops from a life-time of shared experiences. Like a fine wine, their friendships grow sweeter and more precious as time passes. As you begin to listen to tales of his childhood days, you will begin to unfold the paradox that lies beneath the surface of every memory that he has shared so openly in this project. Having fun as family and friends is a priority to Tony, and that night in a downtown restaurant as I sat among many of them, was no different. Throughout the many changes of the last nine years, one thing that has remained a constant is the fun Tony has always had, and will always have with those he calls friends.

Happy, fun, great—are all words Tony uses to describe his childhood. *"We were pretty poor, but we had everything that we needed growing up, and that is all that mattered."* I looked up from my computer screen noticing Tony let out a sigh, while taking a momentarily long pause from the conversation. The timing allowed me to see him wipe away tears just before stating, *"I was extremely blessed as a child. Mom and Dad were good people. They worked hard, and they were always there for my brother Roy and me. If I was playing a ball game or doing anything else in the community, I could count on my Mom being there to root me on as always. Dad would also be there when he did not have to work. Today, many children do not have that privilege."*

As a child Tony portrayed an awkwardly, hazardous type personality. He simpered, *"It appears that I was extremely accident prone. I broke my left arm, and then I re-broke it two more times inside the cast."* Putting his hands behind his head and leaning back into the chair he smiled, *"The family doctor told me the last time that I broke it—If you break this arm one more time—I am going to have to cut your arm off!"*

In addition, Tony admits that he had broken eight toes as a child. *"Mom always described me as an independent little cuss. She said that when I was two years old that I grabbed the spoon and wanted to feed myself. I didn't want anyone else to help me do anything. Mom told Cheryl when we started dating that you can ask Tony to do anything for you, but you can't tell him to do it because he'll never do anything for you."*

Many of Tony's friends and family define him by

using these three distinguished words; "good ole boy." Since childhood, bird dogs have always been an important part of Tony's life. His Dad was a quail hunter, something passed down from generation to generation. To this day, it is not uncommon to see Tony out in the kennel with his beloved bird dogs, caring for them and affectionately patting them on their heads as he is in the process of feeding them or cleaning up their pens. His mom had a little house dog when he was a young child, but the bird dogs were always his pets, and to this day he continues to raise pointer bird dogs.

Like most boys his age, he spent many a summer day out on the baseball field playing his favorite sport. When Tony reminisces about these days a grin appears on his face from ear to hear, and a particular gentleness becomes his features lending to fond memories. As a young boy, he was a pitcher and a catcher and his baseball idol was none other than Mickey Mantle. So, it goes without being said that his favorite team of all time is the New York Yankees. Anytime the league opened up for the season, Tony made sure he got the number seven jersey; the same number Mantel wore throughout his career.

Tony began to snicker when recalling a story about his aunt named Joyce. It wasn't too difficult for me to believe the account after Tony told me what took place when the unsuspecting Joyce came to his home. The first time that she came for a visit, he was about two or three years old. Joyce came into the family after marrying his dad's younger brother. Every time the unsuspecting woman would turn her back on the toddler, Tony would sink his teeth into her. Although his aunt Joyce tried not to take it personally, she admitted that she hated coming to family reunions because of it. She honestly thought the little tot would never outgrow his facetious nature, but he finally did, to some degree.

As the years passed, Tony went to Winnsboro High School and enjoyed studying math because it came easy to him. He never was into sports like his older brother Roy Glynn, the star football player in college. However, he played some, and decided he did not care for it as passionately as farming. In addition, he was in school clubs such as FFA, and Student Council. Tony was the Vice President of the Senior Class and voted the Class Favorite and WHS Nominee. His favorite bands of the day were ZZ Top, the Rolling Stones, and like most young people his age, he was a huge Elvis Presley fan.

After the first day of our meeting, the sun began to set, and Tony appeared to have settled into the routine of me asking questions and so he began approaching the project a bit differently and more relaxed. Once the sunset occurred, the only light on the patio was my computer screen. Tony was oblivious to that, and it did not matter to me either, because his story was so interesting. When we finished for that night, Cheryl mentioned the need to turn on the light so that we could see to get inside.

I laughed when Tony said, *"Why didn't you all say something? I can't see how dark it is."* Giggling at his response, we all sauntered towards the kitchen to grab a bite to eat. Rudy, faithfully by his side, guided him through the house. Rudy is a beautiful shepherd that is rather tall and lengthy for his breed. His eyes are beautifully alert and he carefully guarded the space around his master. He warmed up to me pretty quick, and I to him. Cheryl was finishing up a few things for the meal as Tony continued to tell me about high school days and one very impressive role model who changed the course of his life.

Ms. Burkham, Tony's senior English teacher, was a highly influential figure during his teenage years. She stayed in touch with him many years following school until her death several years ago.

Tony continued, "You see, in Winnsboro, you had to take four years of English to graduate. She was the one who stood at the end of the line when you graduated, and to be able to walk across the stage and receive your diploma you had to go through her."

Ms. Burkham was tall and slender and always dressed extremely conservatively. Her auburn-brown hair was a far contrast to what students called her "expression of steel." Similar to Moses parting the Red Sea, Ms. Burkham beheld the same reputation as she walked the high school hallways. She not only earned the respect of her students—her stance demanded it.

Tony expressed, "Growing up in Winnsboro, there was one thing about me that everyone knew. I was never intimidated or humbled. Needless to say, when I entered the 12ᵗʰ grade she taught me what humble, intimidating, and submissive was all about."

Crow admits that it did him a world of good to have her as a teacher. It only took one intimidating look from her, and he would straighten up immediately. She had that kind of presence, and she took her job seriously in getting students prepared to leave high school and face the future prepared.

When Tony was asked to share his life-changing story at church nine years ago, they asked him to invite people who had impacted his life, and so he called Ms. Burkham, who gladly accepted his invitation.

She called the following morning, after attending church and said, *"You never made good grades in school, but on your speech in church yesterday, I give you an "A," and that's good!"* She continued, *"That is the only "A" you ever got, but you got one!"*

Looking back now, Crow says he could have easily become a straight "A" student if he would have given it the effort. However, all he wanted to do was to finish high school and go on to work. Crow was offered a baseball scholarship to attend Tulsa University, but with his lack of interests for college, he declined the opportunity.

Unfortunately, Crow had one other teacher in high school that was on the undeserving end of his ridicule. He regrets, "When I speak to high school students now, I talk about a freshman speech teacher that we literally terrorized."

He did not mix words when he confirmed that they, in all reality, terrorized her. It began from the first day of school that year until Christmas break, when she left and never returned. Crow, aware of his public speaking schedule today, confesses that he wished nowadays that he would have listened to that teacher. After traveling and speaking in front of thousands, he recognizes that he could utilize what she so desperately tried to teach him decades ago.

Crow emphasized, "I share about the saga I

created over my speech teacher with high schools today because I want the kids to know that even though we ran her off, I should have listened to her and learned from her."

Back in high school, Crow was quite socially active and loved FFA because it had to do with cows and farming and the things that he wanted to do when he grew up. Going to school in the fall was slightly aggravating to him because it got in the way of his bird hunting expeditions. It was great to have summers off, but bird hunting season was in the fall, and so it disappointed him as he missed out on many opportunities due to school schedules.

His longtime friend from childhood, John Greer, has remained his best friend all of these years. John resided catty corner from where the Crow family lived. There was a pasture that separated their homesteads, but nothing could have ever separated the duo as friends during childhood or as adults to this day. The tall football player physic of Greer was an instant attraction to the girls in high school, and they fell all over themselves trying to win his affections. John, being the kind of friend that he was, lined up double dates with Crow who admits today, was a bit on the chunky side as a teenager. He knew the only reason girls agreed to go out with him was so they could be near John, who frankly could care less about the entire ordeal.

In Winnsboro, most guys started work at a young age, and Tony Crow was no exception. In fifth grade, he started his first job hauling hay. Without reservation Crow concedes that by far his best job in life was at TXU. He worked at the power plant for twenty-six years. At first he was a Fuel and Ash Operator, and then went to Equipment Operator, before eventually working in the Control Room. Tony admits that the responsibility taken on at TXU allowed him to develop a much-needed discipline in his life. Working in the power industry meant shift work, and it was a part of life to anyone who agreed to the employ. The plant never closed on holidays, weekends, or birthdays. Due to the rigid scheduling, one expected to work while others were off for Christmas holiday.

Crow says, "That alone taught me to appreciate those who could not be home during evenings, or holidays."

Due to the nature of the job, Crow missed out on being able to attend his children's functions as they grew up. If you ask Crow whether he had any reservations about working for TXU, he would say that he regrets not stepping up to a supervisory role when it was offered to him. He did not think that he was suited for the position, nor prepared to take on that kind of responsibility. Looking back now, he realizes that he should have taken the promotion.

After hearing him admit to such things, I realized that Tony previously confessed that he was in no way ready to accept the responsibility of becoming a public speaker, but astonishingly life had a way of persuading him differently.

Though Tony easily talks to strangers today, he has never been what many would call a social hound. As one who enjoys his privacy, he also enjoys being alone. After working long shift hours, all that he wanted to do was to come home and stay away from people. His job today has broadened his horizons allowing him to mix and mingle with people a lot easier than he did previously. It has helped him realize something that many folks are yet to discover by opening up a new perspective and introducing him to what Crow calls the *"real world."*

Crow adds, "Traveling and speaking have opened up so much for me. I've spoken in Alaska, New York, and even California, and everywhere in between, and the reality is that deep down, no matter where you are from, folks are all the same."

CHAPTER TWO

Love, Life, Laughter

As we sat out on the patio one night, Tony expressed how he was grateful that his parents never had to know about his accident. Up to this point, you the reader have no idea just how the accident happened, or how it affected Tony. Don't worry, we will eventually come to that, but for now, sit back and relax and enjoy hearing this life changing story, and some good laughs.

When Tony speaks about his family, he fondly reflects on how he is similar to his Father, who was well-known in the community as "Cotton Crow." He admits he has some of his mothers' personality, but folks say Tony is *Cotton Crow Junior* all over again.

After Tony was older, his brother, Roy Glynn, moved away while Tony remained in the small farm community that he had grown to love, and where he was most comfortable living. Roy Glynn came for visits such as holidays, and he always stayed with Tony and his family. Their parents would come to Tony's home for all the festive holidays and events as well, meaning that their home was the central gathering place for the family. During those years, Tony became particularly close to his father, and anyone trying to come between them would be hard-set to succeed. His father lovingly called him "Bud", and it was evident that Tony was not only fond of his father but that the admiration and respect was reciprocated.

For instance, Tony recalls, "My Daddy had an operation one day, and he told my brother, 'Go home and take care of our mom and Bud is going to stay here with me'".

Roy Glynn always got called by his full name due to the fact that other family members such as an uncle and granddaddy went by the family name Roy, as well. Now days, it is nothing for Tony and Roy Glynn to speak on the phone two to three times a week. Their relationship has developed into a much closer one since the accident, regardless of how indifferent they were as children.

On June 3, 1978, Tony married his life-mate and confidant Cheryl (Robinson) Crow. At the time of writing this book, they celebrated their 34th wedding anniversary.

Tony smiled and made sure that I heard what he had to say next. "We have had a life-long friendship since we first met in first grade. I have to admit that Cheryl was not my first girlfriend."

Cheryl chimed in, "But I better be his last!"

Laughter burst from the patio table as the three of us responded to her candid remark. After regaining composure, Tony went on to say that he and Cheryl started first grade in the same classroom. They became interested in dating each other when they were juniors in high school. Cheryl admits that she was the first one to ask Tony out on a date. Cheryl said she had been a homecoming nominee, and that she wanted someone to be her escort, so she asked Tony, who was up for the challenge.

Later on, you will see how their engagement was not traditional, but the wedding day was a very special one as Cheryl insisted that they marry in the church she had grown up in and loved. Tony says the wedding was fairly typical, and if you know Tony, he would make sure there was no significant fuss about anything. I do not know how many wives would have sat quietly while their husbands used the word "typical" to describe their wedding, but Cheryl did. I believe most women would have taken offense, but when you meet Tony and Cheryl, neither one of them is about pomp and circumstance, so I took the phrase "typical" to simply mean "not excessive or too fussy" of an affair. This should not be mistaken as "not meaningful or memorable!" Once I framed it that way, I secretly let Tony off the hook.

Their honeymoon was spent in Beavers Bend, Oklahoma. After four days, they had to return home, as Tony insisted he had to get back because his bird dog had just delivered puppies. He was anxious to get home to check on them.

Now, if you are reading this like I am, you may

sarcastically be thinking, "How wonderfully romantic." But once again, you have not seen Cheryl and Tony in action. They are inseparable in every way, and their relationship is built on a lifetime friendship. Not too many people can say that they have known each other all the way through school, fell in love, and then married their best friend. That alone should encourage hopeless romantics in understanding that life is filled with ups and downs and curves and bends in the road. If anyone has encountered the kind of obstacles that this duo has, and navigated their way into the closest and most meaningful relationship available, Tony and Cheryl have. There is an absolute easiness and acceptance that goes unmentioned when you are in their presence. It is kind of like trying on a well-fitted glove that you have had for decades. Nothing feels better than something that has conformed to your hand like a decent working glove.

Romans 8:29 says "For those God foreknew he also predestined to be conformed to the likeness of his Son . . ." (ESV) English Standard Version.

Tony and Cheryl have worked at conforming to the image of Gods' Son, and together the "working glove" needed for their successful marriage has been their love for God and for each other.

Perhaps part of their success is clarified in this simple statement that Tony expressed while we sat out on the back patio. "As far as our relationship, I think it should be Valentine's Day every day instead of just one day a year. I believe a husband needs to show his wife that he loves her daily. I credit Cheryl for the success that I am today."

One night, during my visit, Tony and Cheryl took me dining with some of their closest friends at a local restaurant downtown called, *"Double C."* Back in the day, the same building that was now housing a popular eatery, was once the town feed store. I looked up at the old, rustic, wooden beams and relics that appeared to remain behind the upper banisters that surrounded the entire restaurant. It took seconds to immediately understand the sacrifice and hard work that it took to build this community and make it what it is today. As Benny and Debbie Cowser, Donny and

Phyllis Stone, Cheryl and Tony and I were all seated, we were ready for some story telling. We sat at a raised table with tall chairs in the back part of the restaurant, and it was then that I began to appreciate the unique camaraderie within the group. Once everyone ordered food the conversation took an amusing tone reflecting "back in the day." Things actually came to life when Jeff Zimmerman decided to show up and started sharing musing stories of his adventures with Tony. Now these two characters go way back, and there is no way to predict what might come out of Jeff's mouth when he tells these stories. His dry sense of humor will sneak up and grab you, and the evidence was revealed as the table was full of utter giggles, laughter and smiles once he started in with his mastery, storytelling techniques.

I looked at Tony, and he seemed more than pleased that his buddy Jeff came over to spend some time with us. Immediately they began to harass each other like brothers often do. Perhaps on the surface, you would consider them close friends, but once the stories began, you realize that they have something more than just a friendship bond between them.

Before telling us a story, Jeff smiled and leaned on the table and declared that Tony was the entire time "showing out." Now this term was not anything that I was familiar with, but I soon realized it was likened to the term "showing off." Once I understood it, it appeared to me a bit of an oxymoron for Tony, since he hates to draw attention to himself. On the other hand, when he is relaxed and just having fun with friends, he does reveal a fairly conspicuous side that Jeff invariably has a way of drawing out of him. Just listening to these two characters interact, I thought I was at a standup comedy show in downtown Dallas. Jeff began to relay an event that took place after Tony lost his eyesight, and amongst the outburst of laughter that was far from containable, we the remaining bystanders succumbed to their comedic antics to get us involved in their storytelling. Our involvement turned into leaning forward and not missing a word as these two buddies shared their tales of adventure.

Jeff started in, "Now, Tony knows that I have a

poor sense of direction, and he's the type who remembers every pothole in the road. We were on our way to Mount Pleasant, and we passed the BBQ place, when he asked, 'Is there anybody at the BBQ place?'"

"No, I think it is closed."

After answering him, I was thinking to myself, "Now how does a blind man know that we are near the BBQ place? I can't figure it out!"

"We traveled onward down the road, and Tony stated, 'We ought to be coming near a turn right up here in just a little ways.'"

"About two minutes later we made a turn, and we got over to Mount Pleasant, and Tony starts in again. He asked, 'Aren't we coming up on those railroad tracks?'"

"Sure enough, he was showing out as if he knew where we were the whole time that we were driving. When we got up to the shopping center, I realized that I had enough of it, and I drove into the parking lot. Then I turned the wheel and made a substantial sized donut in the middle of that shopping center parking lot in hopes of throwing him off.

Tony paused and tried to get his bearings and asked, 'Oh, where are we now?'"

"I laughed, 'Well, if you are so smart—you tell me!'"

Those of us sitting at the table burst out in laughter which permeated every square inch of the dining area as we continued to listen to Jeff and Tony's stories.

Tony interjected, "Well—at least I don't run blind men into posts!"

Cheryl looked right at me and grinned, "You'll want to hear this."

Tony looked toward Jeff, and Jeff looked back at Tony and smiled, "Go ahead, tell the story!"

Tony lost no time as he started in, "A few months after I was blinded, Jeff and I decided to go to a country store outside of Winnsboro to eat lunch. After eating and before we decided to leave, we realized that there was probably about twenty guys there sitting and visiting with us. As we were walking out the door, there was a small porch there, and right outside the door in front of us was a post. Well, naturally Jeff just started walking around the post, without saying anything to me. I was holding on to his arm and trusting him to guide me to the vehicle. I was not even aware that the post was in front of me. He just kept walking, and I guess he thought that I would just follow him and sense that he went around that post, but I actually ran right into the center of it. I hit that post so hard that I went down to my knees because it bloodied my nose.

The clincher here is that Jeff did not care about me being hurt. He just started franticly grabbing my arm and saying 'Get up! They're looking at us! Get up!'"

"With all the commotion taking place, the guys inside came out and asked, 'What's going on?'"

I said, "This guy just ran me into the post!"

Once again, those of us listening to the duo lost all composure. Now that they had our undivided attention, the moment continued to escalate as the two of them continued on with more tales.

Tony asked, "Remember when I had a laser put on my deer rifle so that I could go deer hunting?"

"Oh, you're going to tell THAT story—are yuh?" Jeff laughed sarcastically.

Unfazed, Tony carried on, "Well, Jeff wanted to be the first one to take me out deer hunting because, by then, he had become like a mother hen watching over me. Jeff had a deer lease out in Winters, Texas, and we went out there. After we climbed up into the deer stand that afternoon, we assumed how we were going to kill a deer was all figured out.

Later on, that afternoon, we were sitting there and Jeff looked down toward a corn feeder, and announced, 'Hey man—here comes a deer. It's a buck. Get your gun out!'"

"So, I get my gun out, and put my laser on it preparing myself to take down the deer. I think it was a bit too early in the afternoon because the laser had a difficult time working in the bright sunlight.

Jeff piped up, 'It's hard to see that little, red dot out there a hundred yards away or more.'"

"Then Jeff confessed, 'Man, I can't pick it up . . . I can't see your laser!'"

Despite being blind, Tony shot this deer with the help of laser scope.

"We messed around a little bit with it, and because of the way that he was talking, it appeared that he was about to hyperventilate from excitement. I thought this must be a BIG buck.

Referring to my laser, Jeff said, 'Move it over a little bit . . .'"

"Well I tried moving the laser around, and Jeff replied, 'Sorry Tony, but I just can't find it!'"

"I knew by that time that we were going to lose that deer. I thought that he was looking through a pair of binoculars or looking down that way trying to find that deer, and so I replied, 'Don't let him get away, shoot him!'"

"The next thing that I know, I heard an unexpected— POW! I was still holding my rifle, and I heard that loud shot go off. I thought at first that my rifle engaged and that I had accidentally pulled the trigger. Fact is, I never knew that Jeff had a gun with him. I expected him to use my gun if he needed it, not knowing he had packed his own. He had been looking through the scope on his own gun at the deer. What happened is that his scope was directly on that deer, and he could see that my laser wasn't even close to it.

I nervously asked, 'What happened?!!'"

"You said to get him—so I shot him!" Jeff answered.

"You shot my deer?!"

"Well—you said to shoot him!"

"Well, did you get him?"

"Umm . . . yes . . . kind of." Jeff mumbled.

"Jeff, you either got him, or you didn't."

"Well I know I hit him, but I think he took off.

We got to hurry now, because it's getting dark outside."

"I snapped back at him, 'The darkness doesn't bother me Jeff! It's dark to me *all* the time!'"

"So we climbed out of the deer stand, and as we walked out to the corn feeder, he looked and there were some traces of blood.

Jeff said, 'Yes, he is around here somewhere, but man . . . it's getting dark!'"

"Which way did he go?" I asked.

"I heard Jeff say, 'He went around here to the left.'"

"Well, let's go see if we can't track him down and find him."

"So we moved ahead and as we are walking I was holding on to his arm when Jeff mentioned, "Tony, it's really getting dark out here.'"

"I KNOW it is dark Jeff—it's always dark! Don't worry about it. I'll be okay."

"Jeff did not bring a flashlight or anything, and after we walked about fifty yards, with the wind blowing in our face, I asked, 'Do you see him?'"

"No, I don't see him Tony."

"We walked a little further, and I motioned for him to stop."

"What's wrong?' Jeff inquired."

"I took in a deep breath of air through my nose and affirmed, 'I smell that deer.'"

"You SMELL it?"

"Yes, I smell that deer. He is over to our left, so let's just walk over to our left."

"We walked over to the left, and as suspected, the deer lay right in front of us. Jeff shouted, 'You DID smell that deer!'"

"Yeah, well . . . I told you that I did. Is he a big one?"

"Well, not real big." Jeff admitted.

"How big is he Jeff?"

"Insistently, Jeff said, 'Reach down here and you can find out yourself.'"

"So I reached down towards the ground. Now I was expecting to find some antlers or something, but as I put my hand down towards the ground, I could not feel anything."

"Where is he Jeff?"

"Frustrated, Jeff answered, 'You're not feeling close enough!'"

"So I reached further down, and I soon felt the horns—if you can call them that. They were about the size of a pencil and about an inch long."

"'Jeff—This is a baby!' I declared."

"'He's a buck Tony, he's got horns!' Jeff said defensively."

"Well, when we were at the deer stand, you were talking as if he was not only a buck, but a BIG ole buck!"

"It IS dark Tony." Jeff insisted.

"Well, you do know where the truck is—right?" I asked.

"'Yeah, I know where the truck is. I'll go get it.' He disappointedly replied."

Tony smirked, "As little as this thing is, there is no point in going to get the truck. You just pack my rifle, and I will carry the deer."

"I put the deer's four feet together, slung him up over my shoulder, and started walking towards the truck.

"We got to hurry now!" Jeff stated.

"He actually wanted to run. I asked, 'Why are we in such a hurry?'"

I could hear the concern in Jeff's voice when he answered, "My other buddies that I grew up with are coming to the deer camp, and they are supposed to be here very soon. I want this deer skinned and out of the camp before they come. If we don't get it done, I'll never live this down!"

"When we got to the deer camp, we started skinning it, and I told Jeff, 'This is a—Bambi Jeff.' I just kept teasing him."

"Well, Jeff had a buddy, and his name was Tooter, and he said, 'That guy lives up to his name, because he will tell everyone I know about this incident.'"

"Sure enough, right then, Jeff saw headlights coming our direction and commented, 'Here they are!'"

"Tooter got out of the truck and walked up to where we were and instantly questioned us. 'What are you doing killing this baby . . . ? He still has milk around his mouth—for goodness sakes!'"

"Tooter then asked, 'Tony—did you kill this?'"

"No! I had my rifle on him, but good ole Jeff here shot him right out from underneath of me."

"That story got all the way to the power plant, and for days those guys harassed Jeff endlessly. In town people would say, 'There's that guy that shot the deer out from underneath Crow!'"

CHAPTER THREE

I Saw The Light

Once you begin to learn how Jeff and Tony teased each other, you begin to feel at ease around them. There certainly is something out of the norm about this group, and though, this is how friendships should be, you seldom have occasion to witness them in action. I suppose I should not have found it all that unusual, mainly because Tony and Cheryl seemed to do things differently than most couples. For instance, Cheryl proposed to Tony.

I asked Cheryl how that came to pass, and her reply was, "Hey it worked, and we have been married now for 34 years!" She giggled and continued, "By the way, if I get mad at him, I just move the furniture around."

I observed that Tony tends to have a lot of

longtime friends, and that speaks volumes for any person. It also instills a sense of solidarity that many superficial relationships have yet the opportunity to build. Most of the people that Tony hangs out with are friends from his childhood or early adult years. He still goes to the same church that he went to as a teenager and everyone there knows who Tony Crow is and admires him.

After witnessing the faith of Tony Crow, I was curious enough to ask him about his beliefs and how he came to be the person that he is today. He gladly shared how his faith has been pertinent in carrying him through the years. Tony was raised in God fearing home, but his family did not go to church. He speaks of his mama being a deeply spiritual person who met with some people who had church in their homes. There was nothing particularly unordinary about Pearl Crow. She wore her hair up and would never consider wearing much make-up whatsoever. Tony was candid in saying he found nothing appealing about going to church at someone else's house.

It wasn't until he was a junior in high school and started dating that Cheryl finally found a way to get him in church. At first, he did not have a desire to go, and made up excuses to get out of it as much as possible. Cheryl kept asking him and he insisted he was not going.

Sometime later, that same church had a revival meeting. First Baptist Church of Winnsboro was promoting a dynamic speaker named David Stockwell. This man was speaking at high schools everywhere throughout the nation. Back then it was acceptable to mention God in the school arena. The speaker played football for Rice University. As he spoke at the school, he shared more about his football stories than anything else, so as to peak interests in the kids in hopes to have them attend church that night. Tony admits that he did not attend services that first night by successfully worming his way out of the whole ordeal. The second night of the meeting he had an obligation to feed a woman's cows after school. He told Cheryl that he could not come to church because he would be feeding cows way too late. Cheryl put her plan into full gear and decided one way or another; she was going to get Tony Crow to church. She talked to a couple of Tony's best friends, and they came and helped him feed the cows that night so that he could make it to church. After all, what was he going to do after that kind gesture? He had run out of excuses, and so he found his way to church that night. Tony was too nervous to say much to anyone at the services. He says he shares that with others, because he wants them to know that he understands the first timers' apprehension when going to church.

When the end of the service came, Tony was under conviction. He knew that he needed to make a decision, and that meant walking down front and talking with the preacher. Tony admits that it was the Lord and Him only that compelled Tony to go down to that altar that night, and it was there that he decided to make Jesus the Lord of his life. He was seventeen, a junior in high school, and ever since then, he has been attending the same church.

Crow admits that he found Christ, but after marrying Cheryl they stopped going to church for a while. He was working at the power plant, and he only had one Sunday off a month, so he found another excuse for not taking his wife to church. After their daughter, Candace was born and grew old enough, Tony said they wanted her to be in church, so they started going to church regularly again. It also helped that he was also on a different work schedule that permitted him to be off two weekends a month.

Due to the warmth of the Sunday school class, and the teacher, who was a guy that Tony grew up with, Cheryl and Tony developed a sincere love for their church family. Since then, they became faithful members and have never turned away from serving God in their community.

With all that being said, Tony was asked several times if he would consider becoming a deacon of the church. Tony emphatically answered, *"Absolutely not!"*

He wanted nothing to do with that because he perceives it as too much responsibility for the church.

Afterwards, he was in the tragedy that took his sight away, and now he has plenty of time to pray and focus on the things of God. His faith continues to hold him through the journey, and he now has an entirely different perspective on life.

Tony interjected, "It was my Christian friends and family that smothered us with love and care afterward, and that made a tremendous difference to me."

Tony says God spoke to him one day when he was trying his hardest not to talk about the accident. He never thought he would be standing in front of people sharing his story. He admits the last thing on his mind was talking to others about his misfortune, but folks just kept on encouraging him to speak. Tony's aspiration was to stay on the family farm and do what "Tony" wanted to do.

However, one day he sensed the Lord speaking to him: "Tony, just come with me, just walk with me. Let me show you what I have for you."

Crow admits that he knew he was not a speaker, but the journey that the Lord has taken him on in the last four years is one of those "off the chart deals", as Tony would put it.

It fathoms Tony to imagine that he is traveling and speaking all over the United States. He often says he is just a country boy from East Texas that talks like a hick and acts like a hick, yet he stands in front of crowds in New York and finds it inconceivable that they like what he has to say.

Crow says the accident has made him recognize that he now reads people from the heart, instead of through his eyesight. It has made him put his faith in God instead of his own capabilities. He has the wisdom to know that most commonly, people want to do things their own way, and it's when things are going well, folks rarely put their faith in God.

Crow continues, "I once heard it put this way; the wind is blowing, and you can feel it, and you know it's there, but have you ever seen the wind blow? You see the results by the leaves blowing on the trees. This is what blind faith is about. You can't see God, but you know He's there, and you can sense His presence.

There is a scripture in the bible that says, 'For we walk by faith, not by sight;' (2 Corinthians 5:7) KJV.

I got the second part of that down, and I have been working on walking by faith now for nine years, and I can honestly say that nothing has ever been more challenging."

Lights Out!

Tony was ready to move on to the part of the interview where he began to recollect and tell the story about the day he lost his eyesight. One could easily figure out that it was something that he had shared several times before. Each time he tells his story, you could only assume that he has also relived the incident over and over again. After getting to know Tony, I understand that he would never want people to feel sorry for him, nor would he want people to *not ask* him about the tragedy. He truly believes that the reason why the accident happened to him was so that he could be the 'watchmen on the wall', so to speak, forewarning others that accidents change lives forever. I consider myself fortunate to have heard the story in part and in whole over three times, whether by Tony himself, or by a professional

DVD used in his business to communicate the importance of safety at work and at home. This is Tony's recollection of the dark day that took his sight away.

Tony opens his presentation with, "Darkness . . . , total darkness. You could not close your eyes tight enough to see the darkness that I see today. I see absolutely nothing."

Shortly after the tragedy people would ask Tony to share his story, but he always insisted that it was too personal. After several months, Cheryl asked him something that changed Tony's entire outlook.

She inquired, "You know, if you could tell your story, and you could save one family the grief we have had to go through, wouldn't it be worth it?"

Tony admits that her deep conviction in helping others avoid the horrible pain that they had experienced convinced him, and he emphatically replied, "I'll do it . . . I'll do it!"

Tony has come a long way, considering the fact that he initially refused to share his story when the accident happened to him. He now enjoys telling the story, because he realizes how his experience has been able to change so many lives in a positive way.

Before he starts speaking at conferences, he always initiates the audience by saying, "I am so glad to be here to share my story with you today, but I want to make sure that you are comfortable with me being here, so I always tell this story about something that happened to me about four years ago. A friend of mine called me, who was an associate pastor who lives in the Mansfield, TX area, and said, 'Tony, I want you to come over and help my pastor with a sermon.'"

"I replied, 'Well, I'll do my best. I'll certainly try.'"

"He wants you to come up on stage and help him with the sermon. He is going to preach a sermon on spiritual blindness, and he wants to compare physical blindness to spiritual blindness."

"Well, I can take care of my part, if the pastor can take care of his part, there's no doubt about that!" I replied.

"So Cheryl and I went over to his church that

morning, and I told the pastor, 'When we get up there, say something to break the ice a little bit. The children out there might be uneasy about me being in the blind world.'"

"Okay, I can do that." The pastor said.

Meanwhile, the preacher started telling this story, and Tony did not know if it was a joke or not.

"The preacher's wife got a call from her nephew saying, 'I am getting married.'"

"She said, 'That's wonderful news!'"

"The nephew continued 'But before you meet my fiancé, I want to let you know that she has lost an arm.'"

"The preacher's wife said 'That's not a problem, no problem at all.'"

"Now about that time the preacher's son was about four or five years old. All of us know about those four or five year old boys and what is likely to come out of their mouths at the wrong time. So a couple of weeks before they met, she is just pounding her son, 'Don't you even look at that lady! Don't you even say a word to that lady, understand?!'"

"She could just imagine what would come out of his mouth. A couple of weeks pass by until they meet. The little boy is doing exactly what his mom had said. He is hiding behind his moms' leg and not looking at the lady, and he's not saying a thing.

As they visited the one arm girl remarked, 'Your son sure is shy, what is his problem?'"

"The preacher's wife said, 'Don't worry, as soon as he gets to know you, he'll just talk your arm off.'"

"The church broke out in laughter. After we finished with the service, the preacher's wife came up to me and said, 'Tony, I cannot believe that I said that! I meant to say 'ear' and 'arm' rolled right out of my mouth!'"

"The only reason that I tell that story is to let you know about the one armed girl, and that there is nothing funny in that she lost her arm. In fact, it is not anymore funny that I have lost my eyesight. But it is something that has been dealt to us in life, and we have to live with it. I am sure if I could ever talk to that one armed lady, she would view her loss of an arm in the same way that I view my loss of eyesight.

It's much better to smile about it than to frown about it, and it is much better to laugh about it than it is to cry about it."

Tony admits that he would never tell anyone that it is a good thing that he is blind. In fact, he would love to see again. Regardless, he knows that he must go on and live life to its fullest. When you meet Tony, you quickly recognize his *"I'm never going to give up"* attitude. Before the accident, he was much the same, as he has never been a quitter. Anyone who knows Tony says it is his spirit in overcoming obstacles in life that has kept him going. Tony says that it would not be fair to him or to his family to give up, so he will never give up.

Two years after Tony graduated from high school, he was offered a job at a large utility company. He worked at a coal-fired power plant. The first day he reported for work, the foreman in charge of the new hires issued him three items consisting of a hard hat, safety glasses and hearing protection. Going through school, and being an avid hunter, Tony admits that he never heard the word "safety" brought up in his life.

Even at the few odd jobs that he worked while he was still in high school, he never had any supervisor or employer consider talking to him about safety. Their primary concern was getting the job done, not worrying about safety.

After issuing three new hires safety equipment, the foreman took them out on the plant for a tour, and the first thing he mentioned was the importance of safety. This concept was foreign to Tony, especially coming out of the environment that he was used to working in. Repeatedly, throughout the day, the foreman kept teaching about safety, and what a dangerous place the power plant was to be working at. After a few hours went by, Tony wasn't so sure if he wanted to work there anymore.

On Sunday in November of 1993, it became a day that Tony says he will never forget. He was at work when one of the units was down due to an outage. There was a 750 foot concrete stack that stood out behind that unit, and like *Humpty Dumpty*, it came tumbling down in a fury. That stack fell and missed Tony by a mere 50 feet. That was an earthshaking moment for Tony. After getting the go ahead to move, they discovered how many people had gotten injured, and then found out that one man had been killed in the accident. It was a horrible day. The company told the rest of the employees that they could call their families and tell them that they were okay.

When Tony arrived home that day, Cheryl asked, "How bad was it?"

He sadly informed her that it was the worst day of his life. After being home that day and thinking about the accident, much like a rerun in his mind, he said, "You know . . . , I feel like I dodged a big bullet today."

Tony has always believed since nothing happened to him that day, even though the odds were against him, that it was not meant for him to be hurt or killed, and he obviously felt good about that.

Fast forward to ten years later and Tony discovered the truth; being that he was not bullet proof. On a cold winter West Texas day in 2003, he and his son Landon decided to go on an end of the year quail hunt. Hunting was something that Tony had grown up doing, and he instilled the same joy of the sport in Landon his son, who was now seventeen and a junior in high school. Some of the best days that they had together were spent out in the fields flushing out birds with their bird dogs. They decided to go hunting on February 14th, Valentine's Day. Tony always makes that comment when he is speaking, especially when he gets to that part of the story, he says that he can feel the heat from the front row coming off the women's faces as they disgustingly think, "How dare you to go hunting on that day."

Like many men enjoy golfing and fishing, Tony's passion has always been hunting, and now Landon had come to admire the sport as much, if not more than his father. As they were headed out to West Texas on the hunting trip, they drove up on the back side of a truck and Landon said, "Hey dad, look! They're going hunting too."

Tony came to the same decision, as he had seen the dog boxes in the back of the truck. Nevertheless, as soon as they started to pass the truck, it was not the dog boxes or other things that caught Tony's eye, but it was the guy actually driving the truck. As he was driving down the road, he had his arm up on the window ledge of the pickup truck door. Tony immediately noticed that the man had on a bright orange hunting shirt, and it really caught his eye. He remembers thinking how ridiculously bright it was and made a remark to Landon that he wishes he could take back to this day. What he said reflected the true image of his mindset back then.

He said to his seventeen year old son, "They must be city slicker bird hunter's son . . . , they're wearing orange." They both chuckled at that as they passed on by the supposedly inexperienced hunters.

Tony had no idea where the men were from. He considered the fact that if someone had to go out and buy clothing just to go hunting, and to insure that their hunting buddy could see them, they must be inexperienced city slickers. Tony never gave a second thought about the khaki shirt he was wearing, as it was always what he wore when he went hunting, and therefore, he never instilled the importance of safety into Landon either. His mindset was that work was one thing, but leisure time falls into a whole different category.

Tony and Landon were able to hunt on February 14th, and it was great. The very next day, February 15th, was cold and overcast, but otherwise supreme hunting weather for bird hunting. They had the hunting dogs out and ready for the tasks, and on they went to the familiar place they had been numerous times before. The hunt went perfect as planned, that is until about 3:00 that afternoon. They had taken a break to eat lunch, and decided to go out for one more hunt afterward. Landon soon had spotted a covey of quail going up an old abandoned fence row, as often seen in West Texas. West Texas is notoriously famous for mesquite trees, and they usually only grow up to about chest high on an average sized man. If you are standing behind them with a khaki shirt and cap on, you can blend in perfectly, causing an instant blinder from your prey. As they took off towards that scattered covey up the old fence row, Landon was standing over to Tony's right, which was only about 75 feet away.

Tony hollered at Landon, "I'm heading up the fence row."

About that moment, a dog pointed straight in front of Tony. The dog had spotted the quail, and he had pointed his nose right in front of Tony as he was starting up the fence line. Tony, caught off guard, lost his chain of thought, and forgot that he had told his son that he was headed up the same fence row.

Putting it in Tony's words, he said, "I had taken my mind off business." He then poses the question, "How many times have you been in safety meetings, or at work, and been told to make sure that you communicate? We are reminded constantly to make sure that other workers know where we are located."

Tony had just told Landon that he was headed up the fence row, but the quail flew up and headed back towards Tony exhibiting a mind of their own. Landon, expecting his father to be on up the old fence row, then turned and focused on what he thought was a bird in his gun sites. Remember, Tony's clothing camouflaged him perfectly, and the quail flew up over Tony's head. Never seeing Tony standing in front of him, Landon turned and let off a round from his 12 gauge shot gun, hitting Tony directly in the face.

Tony recalls, "I went from uncorrected 20-20 vision to lights out, just like that!"

Instantly, Tony collapsed on the ground as everything went dark, and he could hear his son running through the bushes and crying out, "Oh my God daddy, what have I done!"

Once Landon reached his dad, Tony answered, "Son, you need to get me to the hospital."

Though he was not considered a big framed boy at seventeen, Landon helped Tony up, put two shotguns on his back and helped Tony to the truck, which was a half of a mile down the road. When they got to the truck, they called Birdie and Bobby Jo Helton, the friends they had stayed with the night before in Knox City, TX. After finding out from them where to go, Landon drove fifteen miles, to what was known back then as a very small hospital. When Tony arrived at the place that was more like a medical clinic, they had already called in a care flight helicopter because they knew they could not help him, especially someone in such serious condition.

Immediately a helicopter was there to take Tony on to Abilene, TX. They loaded Tony up in just minutes and flew that way. When he arrived in Abilene, all that Tony could hear was the muffles of people talking.

The friends that they were staying with in Knox City had called their eye doctor and told him, "You've got to get to the hospital and check on Tony."

Tony said he just knew that the doctor was shining a light into his eyes when he asked, "Can you see this? Can you see that?"

Tony replied, "No."

At that time, Tony was clueless about the outcome of the accident, never realizing that he would be permanently blinded for life. His eyes kept burning like they were on fire, and he kept feeling what he thought were tears coming out of them, and running down his face. He thought he would eventually be able to see once his eyes stopped watering.

At last, the doctor spoke up to the Care Flight Unit and said, "Don't leave. We've got to get this guy out of here. This is way out of our league."

Hendricks hospital in Abilene, Texas is a decent sized hospital, so Tony began to realize that his condition was more critical than he first anticipated. The doctor ordered, "We've got to get him to Dallas, TX to Parkland Hospital's Trauma Unit."

Landon and their friends had not arrived yet, because they were seventy-five miles away when the helicopter took Tony on to Abilene. A million thoughts went through Tony's mind as he was lying there all alone. "Parkland Hospital . . . Dallas—and I'm shot." It was 2003 and suddenly Tony remembered that forty years ago, back in 1963, President Kennedy was shot in Dallas, and they took him to Parkland Hospital Trauma Unit. Regardless of the pain he was experiencing at the time, Tony's sense of humor always carries him through.

He says, "I tell people all the time, while lying in that hospital bed, my thoughts were, 'I hope those doctors have gotten better over there in the last forty years.'"

Shortly afterward, he could hear Landon, Birdie and Bobby Jo arrive. Within minutes, the hospital transport team loaded him on the medic chopper and flew him out to Parkland Hospital. During that flight, they sedated Tony, and he went to sleep.

Upon arrival to Parkland Hospital, the triage personnel began doing what they do best. The doctor assessed Tony and realized that he would need surgery.

Tony still could not see anything. He kept saying if the tears would stop running and just clear from his eyes, maybe he would be able to see again.

It was then that the doctor gently informed him, "Mr. Crow, those are not tears that you are feeling on your face, that is blood."

The next thing he remembers is awakening to a wonderful smell. He was in an ICU hospital room, and he could smell something in his room. Though he could not see or hear anyone, he smelled a beautiful perfume.

Speaking up he asked, "Is there someone in

here?"

He then heard a woman's voice respond, "Oh yes, Mr. Crow. How did you know that I was in here?"

"I could smell you." Tony answered.

"Do I smell bad?" she asked.

"No, you smell wonderful! That perfume smells great!"

Through the years, people ask Tony if his other senses kicked in when he lost his sight. He tells them that particular story and then asked them, "Does that answer your question?"

The nurse then continued, "I have some questions that I need to ask you. Do you know where you are at?"

"Well, I think I'm in Parkland Hospital"

She said, "That's right. One more question."

"Sure . . . go ahead."

"Well, there is just one question I am dying to ask you. Right before you woke up; you were muttering something about an orange shirt. Do you think you have an orange shirt on?"

Tony answered, "No, but I sure wish I did!"

"What's the deal with the orange shirt, Mr. Crow?" the nurse pressed.

"I'll tell you that story later," he replied.

Momentarily, the doctors arrived, and as they were shining light into Tony's eyes again they asked, "Can you see this?"

Tony became frustrated and fired back. "Doc? Am I ever going to be able to see again?"

There was no answer, and so Tony asked a second time, getting a little gruff with the doctor. Again, there was no response.

Finally, Tony spit out, "I answered your questions, now you answer mine. Am I ever going to be able to see again?!!"

After he asked the question the third time, the doctor finally relented, "No Tony, you'll never see again."

"Okay." Tony slowly responded.

Tony could not believe that is how he responded. "There hasn't been one thing *okay* about this entire ordeal." I understood what he was saying, and I finally realized that I would never see again.

After the finality of that moment sunk in, the doctors walked out and Tony could smell that perfume again.

"Nurse?" Tony inquired.

"How do you know that I am here?" the puzzled nurse asked.

"I can smell your perfume again."

She was so surprised at that, but she said, "Mr. Crow, I got a few more questions that I need to ask you."

Tony thought to himself, "Here we go with the one hundred and one inquisitions."

"Mr. Crow, are you a celebrity or something?"

Laughing out loud, he chuckled, "A celebrity?! I don't even know how to spell celebrity. What are you talking about? The closest thing that I will ever be to a celebrity is that I am married to Cheryl Crow. (*He was reminding her about the music star named Sheryl Crow)* That's pretty close. So tell me what are you talking about?"

The nurse explained, "Well are you the mayor of your town?"

"Ma'am, I don't even live in town, I live out in the country."

She continued, "You know, I have worked here for twenty years in the Trauma Unit and I have never seen that many people in the waiting room in all my life. I am going to go out there and count them, and I will be right back."

So in a little bit, Tony smelled the same perfume as she arrived and he responded, "You're back?"

The nurse shockingly replied, "Yes, Mr. Crow and there are about seventy-two people in the waiting area."

"Seventy-two people . . . ? There aren't seventy-two people in the world that like me enough to come all the way to Parkland Hospital."

Then the gravity of the situation struck him as things began to make sense of the incident. He realized for the first time that this accident was not just about him. And like a mantra, that thought kept being replayed in his mind over and over again, "It's not just about me . . . it's not just about me . . ."

That is where the acronym INJAM eventually

came from. This accident affected his family, friends and coworkers. Though he could no longer see a visible light, darkness began to clear his minds' eye, and he realized that all of those people weren't just there at the hospital to see Tony Crow. As complementary as it first sounded, he was in ICU, and back then no one was permitted to visit that secure part of the hospital.

Tony addresses the audience, "Who do you think those people were there for?"

Then he explains, that for one, they were there trying to help his wife, Cheryl Crow. Secondly, his daughter was a junior in college and his son Landon, was a junior in high school. Both had many of their friends out in that waiting area offering support to them and helping in any way possible to lessen the grief.

Tony pensively acknowledged, "Those seventy-two people were out there trying to help my family! This accident that happened is a whole lot bigger than Tony Crow!"

When Tony shares his story he usually asks the

audience, "How many times have you asked yourself 'Hey, if I get hurt on the job, who is it going to affect other than me?' If that is your conclusion, it's time to wake up. It is more than just about YOU . . . accidents change lives forever."

As Tony laid in ICU, he could imagine what his wife was thinking as she was outside in the waiting room. He knows she is thinking, "My son has just shot my husband, and my husband will be blind the rest of his life."

He could only imagine what kind of thoughts were going through his daughter's mind. *"I'll never be able to finish college 'cause daddy will never be able to work again."* Then the final one, as he could not even bear to think what his son was coping with, *"I've shot my daddy, and he is going to be blind the rest of his life."*

Tony called out, "I want to get up."

The nurse came to his side, "Mr. Crow, we can't let you get up out of bed. You are strapped into that bed for now. You see, there is a bee-bee that went through your left eye and directly into your brain.

The doctors are concerned that it is going to cause seizures, so you cannot get up at this time."

Now, Tony had something else to worry about. He thought to himself, "How long am I going to be blind? Am I going to have problems with seizures the rest of my life?"

After several days, the doctors decided that it was better to leave the bee-bee on the brain, than to try and remove it surgically. To this day, Tony has been extremely grateful that he has not had any issues with it.

About a week later, they decided that they were going to put Tony in a private room. What started happening next even took Tony by surprise. The phone started ringing off the wall morning and night. Most of those people were co-workers that he had worked with at the power plant for twenty-six years. The accident affected his co-workers in an unbelievable way. They had a distinctive way to look at the whole situation, and that was as if *"one of their own"* had gone down. After working with people for that many years, Tony naturally developed relationships with them, and their families. They raised their children together, and everyone knew everyone else in a close way due to their family environment. They knew that not only did Tony lose his eyesight but that Landon had shot him, which made them look at it the accident as a double tragedy.

The incident really upset the workers at the power plant, and they would call and ask how Tony was doing. Tony would always respond, "I'm going to be blind the rest of my life, but I am going to be okay."

Every single one of them started crying on the telephone. The accident had affected all of them, as well. Tony could not recall one time that he had ever seen one of those guys shed a tear, and so to have them become so emotional over his loss, genuinely moved him. The funny thing is that when these co-workers would call to console Tony, he would eventually end up consoling them in turn, because the accident affected them so deeply.

One buddy, his own supervisor, called Tony at 2:00 in the morning. Cheryl asked, "Why are they calling you this time of the night?"

Tony smiled and answered her, "Don't you remember? I used to work at this time of the night. They're calling from work."

So, the guy that called said, "We got it all figured out here at the power plant. We are going to get you a dog."

". . . A dog?" Tony replied.

Tony admits that as he was laying there in Parkland Hospital, that the furthest thing from his mind was getting a dog. He jolted back, "I got bird dogs. What do I need another dog for?"

"We're talking about a seeing eye dog." His buddy explained.

"Oh—really?"

Tony goes on to explain to me, "Now I love this guy to death, but I honestly think he was thinking that you could go down to the local Wal-Mart and buy one of these dogs. You know what I mean? He could bring a dog up to the hospital, and I could walk right out of there and everything was going to be wonderful! Every time this guy called me and started talking about getting me that dog, I would remind him that I think there is a little more to it than what he expected."

Fact is, it affected him personally, and he wanted to help Tony so much, and so, the only way he knew how to help, was to get him a dog.

After several days passed, you would think that Tony was able to forget the guys wearing the orange hunting shirts, but think again. In quiet moments at the hospital, when all he could do was lay and think, he became ashamed of how he made fun of those hunters that morning as they were wearing orange hunting shirts.

After several days of being in the hospital, the doctor said, "Tony, I don't think it would do any good to operate on your eyes, but we can never close the door on this until we give it a try. I do not think that operating will give you any kind of sight, but if we do not try, you will always wonder, and I'll wonder, if you could have ever gotten any of your vision back. Just so you know Tony, I am not talking about driving home. I am talking about being able to see if it is daytime or dark outside."

Tony's response was, "Hey . . . , I don't have anything to lose."

"That's right Tony. You've got nothing to lose. You have nothing lose, but only *something* to gain."

They went on to explain why they were going to operate at Parkland on his right eye because it was in better shape than the left one. The first thing the doctor said after explaining the procedure was, "Hope for a long operation."

Tony's brows furled a question, "Why?"

"The longer I am in there, the more of a chance it is going to work." The doctor answered as he prepared to get set up.

Minutes before Tony went into the operation, he asked the nurse, "What time is it?"

She said, "Don't ask that question."
Then he said, "Ma'am . . . tell me what time it is."

She reluctantly replied, "It's 8:30 in the morning."

After the procedure when Tony awakened from the anesthesia, the first thing he asked was "What time is it?"

"Oh, I don't know . . ." the nurse hem-hawed around.

"Ma'am . . . please tell me what time it is."

"It's about 9:30 a.m."

His mind drew the dismal conclusion. Though he was disappointed, he was glad that they had tried. Minutes later the doctor walked in to apologize, "Tony, I'm sorry."

Tony then began consoling the doctor, "Don't worry about it Doc. You did the best that you could do, and that is all anyone could expect."

Cheryl piped up and asked "Doc, if Tony would have had safety glasses on, would it have blinded him?"

"No Mrs. Crow, it would not have blinded him. Any kind of good eye wear would have reflected those bee-bees off his eyes, and he would not have been blinded."

Tony recalls back to the time when he was first going to work at the power plant, and the foreman issued him a pair of safety glasses. Tony wore those safety glasses religiously. The problem, however, is that Tony never thought about safety outside of the plant. Tony admits that he never learned the true value of safety until he was blindsided. He would walk outside the workforce, take a chance, roll the dice—so to speak, and hope that it didn't come up snake eyes. In other words, he was two different people; he was cognizant about safety as an employee, but outside of work, he was nothing but a reckless wonder. He was so confident that nothing would ever happen to him away from work, that the concept of being safe, or using safety measures at home or play was the farthest thing from his mind. After all, he tried to approach it logically by saying that nothing could be dangerous away from the workplace.

National statistics reveal that 5-11% of accidents happen away from work, compared to being in the workplace. The reasoning is that there are too many "*Tony Crows*'" who think an accident will never happen away from work, thus, they never think about anything happening in their own backyard. If you still believe that, after hearing this story, then you are missing the entire point. At home, we tend to let our guard down. When we leave work, we feel like we are ten feet tall, and bullet-proof. Tony has proven that we are not ten feet tall, nor are we bullet-proof.

For twenty six years, Tony wore safety glasses daily, but when he went hunting you could just forget it because, in all essence, he was having fun. The critical lesson that he has learned is that safety does not have to get in the way of having fun.

After being released from the hospital, Cheryl drove him home. When they arrived, there were people standing all over their front yard waiting to see Tony. These were the same guys Tony had worked with, and who had also stayed up after their graveyard shifts, just to greet him.

Tony explained, "After Cheryl informed me of the large crowd awaiting us, I said something to my wife that I wished a million times that I could take back. "Send them all home, I don't want to face them."

Cheryl tried to make him understand, "These are your friends Tony!!!?"

"I know, but I feel as if I have let them all down, so send them home. I don't want to face them," he said with shame.

His wife escorted him into the house, and when he got there, she placed his hands on the kitchen counter.

Tony was elated, "Man—what a fantastic feeling to hold on to something knowing that if I turned to the right that I knew where to go, and if I turned to the left, I knew exactly where I was heading."

The entire stay at the hospital left him quite disoriented. He had no idea what end was up. Now, being on home turf, he finally could relax and come to grips with what life ahead was going to be like for him and his family. It was a terrific feeling. He just wanted to soak up the moment as long as possible, and was doing just that until the phone rang.

Cheryl answered it, "Yes, he is right here. I'll let you talk to him."

It happened to be the only blind person that Tony had ever known in his entire life. The man greeted him with, "Tony, welcome to the blind world."

Tony recoiled, "That is not what I wanted to hear!"

He said, "I need to tell you something, from one blind man to another. You need to learn a few blind jokes."

Tony replied, "Jokes? This is no *joking* matter."

Again he answered, "You're just not getting the big picture. You were raised in this little town of three thousand people. They know you and you know everyone, and they will stay away from you because they will be afraid that they'll say something wrong, and I know that you do not want that. Learn a few blind jokes, and tell them to your friends, and they'll know it will be okay."

Afterward, Tony took what this man had said to heart. No one else could have effectively delivered a message with that kind of substance.

"One last thing; before I get off the phone, my wife has brought something to Cheryl, so that she can give it to you. It will be your best friend from days to come."

"It's this cane?" Tony replied as Cheryl handed it

to him.

The man went on without missing a beat, "That will be your best buddy for days to come. I had an extra one so I gave it to you."

As time passed, Tony had an opportunity to talk to his co-workers at the plant. Tony continues to go out periodically to visit them.

Tony said, "I told this one man at the plant who worked in the same control room where I worked the last four years of my employment, that I was scared. The control room is where you start and stop all of the equipment on the plant. I told him what frightened me the most about this job was not learning the logistics of the job, or knowing that I could do the job well. What scared me the most was that it would just tear me up if I were to do something that made someone outside get hurt. That is what my son has to live with the rest of his life. Is my son blind? No, he is not. But he carries such an enormous burden on his shoulders that I would not wish on my worst enemy. So, just because you are not the one that was actually injured, it does not mean that you are not involved in it. I would love to take that burden off my son, but I cannot. If something happens where you work, and you cause someone else to get hurt, you are going to carry that same burden on your shoulders. Frankly, no one wants to do that."

Tony continued, "If I had only been the kind of father that I should have been, I would not have made fun of those guys in orange shirts in front of Landon. On the contrary, I would have insisted that we wear safety glasses and proper hunting gear. My hindsight has become increasingly clearer over the years and I encourage you fathers, as you are reading this to take precautions now to protect not only yourself, but your family. It is your responsibility to initiate safety at work and at home."

Convicted, Tony says, "I tell people today that the only thing I know that is wrong with me is that I am blind. Two weeks after the accident they operated on my one eye, but it was unsuccessful. A few weeks later they operated on my left eye due to the bee-bee hitting it. Six months later, due to the enormous amount of pain that I was encountering in my left eye, doctors finally removed it and gave me a prosthetic eye.

Tony recalls asking the prosthetic eye technician "Is it possible to have a tattoo put on my eye?"

"Yes Mr. Crow," the man smiled.

Tony was extremely pleased to be able to have his favorite scripture, Philippians 4:13 *"I can do all things through Christ that strengthens me,"* and his cattle brand tattooed right on his prosthetic eye. He might not be able to see the actual tattoo, but it stands as a constant reminder that he is not going through this life all alone. He is reminded that how he acts and what he does or doesn't do, directly affects others. Tony carries a new mantra these days, and that is one of a watchman reminding people to take safety seriously, and how important it is never to overlook it, because it only takes a second to be left in the dark. His intention is to make sure that no one on his watch is going to be left in the dark.

CHAPTER FIVE

A Man and His Dog

As time passed, the idea about the guide dog just would not stop. Tony's work friends called him daily to check on him and to keep the idea of the dog in sight. After fourteen long months of being blind, he was able to apply for a Leader Dog for the blind in Rochester, MI, and was accepted. Tony's wife flew with him to Detroit MI. Upon arrival, Cheryl had to deliver Tony to go with a man who was waiting there to pick him up. She will tell you to this day that it was the hardest thing for her to do, and that was to let go of Tony's arm and leave him there with a total stranger. Tony admits that it was the hardest thing that he ever had to do too.

As they were heading out to get on the bus, the man said to Tony, "I want to let you know that everyone on this bus is blind."

Tony smiled, "As I was heading out there, I kept thinking, 'I hope there is *one* person on the bus who was not blind—at least one would help! If not, it's going to be a rough trip.'"

When we arrived at the bus, the man said, "Now, I want you to tell everyone your name and where you are from."

When Tony stepped up into the bus, he said, "My name is Tony Crow from Winnsboro, TX."

Tony recalled the moment. He shared that there is always a wise guy sitting in the back of the bus, and without hesitation, the stranger spoke up, "I never thought you would have been from Texas."

Tony thought, "I suppose he was alluding to my accent."

After his remark, Tony settled in with the assumption that this was going to be the longest month of his life. After they arrived at the facility, he had to train with the same instructor for two days before he was issued a Leader Dog.

Tony's curiosity got the better of him, and he

asked, "Why do you call these dogs, Leader Dogs? I have always heard that places like this had Seeing Eye Dogs, or Guide Dogs, but you call them Leader Dogs. Why do you call them Leader Dogs?"

What Tony's instructor said has been engraved into his mind, and that is why he is so passionate about safety. Simply put, the instructor informed Tony that Rudy was the Leader and that Tony needed to be on Rudy's team. Everything that Rudy had learned for an entire year was strictly about safety, but it will never work unless Tony gets on board and becomes part of Rudy's safety team. There must be an understanding that it takes team work for Rudy and Tony to be successful, or it will never work at all.

Tony reiterated, "I have an opportunity now to talk to companies all over the United States about safety. I always encourage them to understand what leadership and teamwork is all about in the world of safety. There are safety leaders and safety team members, but all employees need to be on the same team for safety to work effectively."

After the third day, they brought Rudy out to meet

Tony. Two Notre Dame Alumni raised Rudy for one year while he was a puppy and then released him back into the program to be trained. When they brought Rudy into Tony's room to meet him, Rudy just got excited and started licking Tony on the face. It was then that Tony knew that Rudy was going to make a difference in his life. Rudy became an attitude changer for Tony. Tony tells audiences everywhere that his father had a way of changing his attitude when he was growing up—and it wasn't by giving him a dog either. Rudy was exactly what Tony needed to cross the bridge that had been holding him back. With Rudy's help, Tony would be able to regain some independence that he had lost by losing his eyesight. Rudy accepted Tony instantly, and in time, their bond became inseparable.

Before Tony could ever qualify to have a leader dog, he had to do some training at home too, and that consisted of walking on the street, crossing streets, and knowing how to maneuver around town with his walking cane. After Tony and Rudy had a day to get adjusted to one another, the real training began. On the fourth day, Tony was instructed that he would be taking Rudy out in town for the first time, and frankly he was a bit unsettled about the whole thing. In Rochester, MI there was a town square where the organization worked. The building was on the square.

The instructor clearly stated, "Okay Tony. Today will be you and Rudy's first time out."

Subsequently, Tony held his composure on the outside, but his heart was beating a million miles an hour as panic washed over him. The reality that he was going to take this dog out in the streets with cars and other traffic was unnerving. All of the sudden it seemed like an impossible feat, but he had signed up for this, so like any good ole country boy who would never think of going back on his word, he pushed himself onward.

The female trainer approached and gave Tony the information needed for the excursion. She stated, "I want you to walk out the front door, go to the curb and turn right, and cross six streets. After you have crossed that sixth-street, turn left to make a block in town and come right back here."

Fortunately, the woman did not know what Tony's thoughts were. His head whirled, "Lady, you have lost your mind!" He was thinking that it sounds easy for her because she can see.

Though Tony was able to contain his deepest fears until that point, the thought of taking a dog out on the square, getting lost, and then being stuck in Michigan forever, was all that was in the forefront of his mind. In the moment of mental crisis, he devised a plan on how to successfully accomplish the mission. He decided to tear off six pieces of paper and put them in his pocket and then off he went.

As Tony crossed a street he decided that he would throw out a piece of paper. Once he ran out, he would have made it far enough to likely get back. To him, it seemed like a feasible plan, and so when he crossed the third street he threw out a piece of paper. What happened next, took Tony totally by surprise.

"Tony, what are you doing?" his instructor asked?

Startled by the voice, Tony was unaware of the trainer's presence. She said, "What are you throwing the paper out on the street for?"

Tony admitted that he was more than nervous about the first excursion and shared his well-planned out theory with her, at no avail. He thought he would forget how many streets he had crossed, be lost in Michigan, and that they would never find Rudy or him again.

The instructor calmly informed him, "Tony, you don't understand. They don't like you littering. I'm right here behind you."

Slightly rumpled, Tony shot back," How is a blind man supposed to know that? You didn't tell me when we left the place that you were going to be walking behind me!"

Afterward, Tony made a complete block with Rudy by his side all the way.

As Tony shared this story, I found myself contemplating about the place he was at physically nine years ago, compared to today. Tony may not have been as spiritually intuitive before he lost his sight, and he has shared many times how his loss of vision has enabled him to see God more clearly. As I heard this part of the story, I recognized the deep contrast to where he is today. He was unaware of the instructor's presence while he walked down the sidewalk with Rudy. However, today, Tony is acutely aware of Gods' presence every time he is outside his comfort zone. He depends on God to take him from Point A to Point B. As Tony devised a plan to maneuver through the training course with Rudy, he has also learned that it is impossible to devise such plans today. He has come to the realization that when you put your trust in God, He will get you home.

Tony learned a valuable lesson that he must trust the Lord, and not depend on his own knowledge or understanding of situations. Proverbs 3: 5-6 says, *"Trust in the LORD with all your heart; and lean not unto your own understanding. In all thy ways acknowledge him, and he shall direct thy paths."* (NIV) The New International Version.

When Tony met Rudy, he knew things were going to be different, but he never imagined at that very moment just how different it would be to allow God to lead him through life, and for him to simply follow.

Later that afternoon, after the first successful training excursion, Tony was allowed to take Rudy out again. As they were walking along, Rudy came to a complete halt. Now when Rudy stops it simply means that he is telling Tony that something doesn't look correct, or that something doesn't seem right here. From that point, it is Tony's responsibility to check out the situation. He stuck his foot out in front of both of them and realized that there was a small puddle of water on the sidewalk. Thinking nothing of it, he reached up to see if a limb from a tree obscured the walkway, or if an awning had come off the building.

Finally, after exhausting all means, he posed the question, "Instructor? What is Rudy stopping for?"

She answered, "He stopped for the little puddle of water on the sidewalk."

"You've got be kidding me! You mean every time there is a puddle of water on the sidewalk, Rudy is going to stop?!!"

She said, "You do not understand. Rudy does not take chances. He does not know how deep that water is, so he will not take a chance of crossing you through it or getting you hurt."

That is when it finally clicked with Tony, and he said, "They can teach a dog in one year of training don't take chances. If it doesn't seem right, don't do it. If it doesn't look right, don't do it—get some help. I went to twenty six years of safety meetings, and I would walk outside and take a chance, (roll the dice) and hope it didn't come up snake eyes. There's something wrong with this deal. Fact is, they can teach a dog in one year of training about how not to take chances, but I could not learn the value of safety in twenty-six years."

A guy asked Tony in one of his meetings, "Tony, are you comparing us to your dog?"

Tony smiled, "No, I'll let you do that."

So Rudy knows if it doesn't look right . . . get help. Who is his help? That would be Tony. Tony communicated to Rudy about the shallow puddle in the sidewalk, and they walked around it. Rudy then went on about his business, protecting, guiding, and warning Tony of impinging danger.

It finally dawned on Tony why they call these dogs, Leader Dogs. Rudy is leading Tony in the safest manner he knows how to lead him.

Tony continued, "How many times do we go back to our work places and tell other people that we need leaders who will lead other people in our workforce to make sure things are safe? That is what Rudy is. He is a Leader, and he doesn't take chances. What a great feeling knowing that when I am crossing a four lane road with eighteen wheelers on it, that Rudy's got my back and that he is not taking any chances. He does it the safe way."

After that day at Leader Dog training, and every day while Tony was there, he would ask his instructor, "Why we are doing things this way."

She would always answer, "It's the *safest* way. All that we have taught Rudy for a year is about safety."

A few weeks passed, and then Tony's family came for a midmonth meeting. His wife walked in the room and gave him a hug and kiss, as did his daughter. However, Landon's response was quite different.

He walked up to Tony and asked, "Dad, where's that dog?"

Tony knew then that life had undoubtedly changed. Landon got down in the middle of the floor and began playing with the dog. It was as if he was a little boy again.

To this day Tony inquires of his audiences, "What do you think this dog represents to my son? I know it represents my eyes. When he sees this dog, he loves him, because he knows that this dog is daddy's eyes."

After just one week, Tony saw Rudy taking full responsibility for Tony and himself. Two weeks later, Tony and Rudy had successfully passed the training course. Tony's family and friends, who had worked so hard to give him something back, now could see him and Rudy walk anywhere independently and do whatever they wanted to do. They knew that Rudy was going to take care of Tony. He was not only going to lead him, but lead him in a safe manner.

Tony explains, "I have yet to have this dog fail me. Wouldn't it be wonderful if we went back to our workforces and knew that we had someone who was not going to let anything happen to anyone because he is a leader?"

When Tony and Rudy came home, it took Rudy about two months to assume responsibilities and to learn the lay of the land at Crow Farms. It was then that Tony felt completely confident in Rudy's ability to get him from place to place safely. It did not take long for Tony to regain some of his independence as Rudy would take Tony anywhere on the farm and return him safely back to the house without an incident.

When he got home and started working on an everyday basis with Rudy, something came back to mind. He began to remember the third item that they issued him when he went to work at the power plant. That noteworthy item was hearing protection. The company he worked for constantly reminded the employees of the value of hearing protection, and encouraged them to use it. They stressed "If you don't use it, you will wish someday that you did."

After getting home with Rudy, and understanding

how vital it was that he had pretty decent hearing, Tony felt relieved about that. He wasted no time in telling others that if he had disregarded the guidance about using hearing protection for twenty-six years at the power plant, that he may be hard of hearing, and blind. Tony calls that, "double my trouble."

Tony emphasized, "Can you imagine what it would be like not to be able to hear or see?" I ask people all the time, 'What do you think I locate things with today?' It's my ears. I can locate a car coming down the street with my ears. One thing that we take for granted about hearing protection is that we don't lose our hearing overnight. If we don't wear hearing protection, hearing loss is a gradual thing, as you won't go deaf instantly. It's very much unlike going blind in one minute. I assure you this, that I worked for an organization that encouraged me to wear hearing protection. Because of it, today I am able to pinpoint with my hearing. I could not imagine what I would have to go through, if I could not hear things today."

After visiting the Crow Farm for a few days, I

was anxious to see Rudy and Tony at work. It was a Saturday morning, and I awakened to birds chirping outside the guest bedroom window. At the Crow Farm it was time for Tony to go out and feed the dogs and the cattle. Tony advised me simply to follow him, and as I did, he and his faithful dog took off ahead. It was then that I learned that Rudy is Tony's *Leader* Dog. I also discovered that Tony's co-workers helped raise money for some of the expenses when it came to obtaining a Leader Dog. In the end, the local Lions Club actually provided the opportunity for Tony to get Rudy.

Rudy appears to be very tall and long bodied for a shepherd. His black and tan marked coat is kept meticulously clean, and he is particularly protective of his master. Though he is large in size, he does not seem to intimidate anyone. His brown bear eyes exhibit a form of dignity and pride as he performs his daily duties. He warmed up to me pretty quickly and as a good host, offered me his belly for a rubbing. He also would give out a kiss or two of approval, and I felt connected to him instantly. It must have been his southern hospitality that seduced my affections.

Tony and his bird dog Jete.

As we took off toward the back of the house, Tony would gently command Rudy as to where he wanted to go. As they approached the gate that opened into the dog yard and out building, fondly called *the man cave*, Rudy guided Tony upstairs to the feed bins. It was quite a sight to see all of the bird dogs in their kennels getting excited about seeing us arrive. Tony began his routine of filling the feed pans. During this time, Rudy's leash was removed, and he was allowed to play with the other family dog that played outside. He would run in circles and play around like any other dog naturally would. Watching Tony navigate through the dog kennel yard was phenomenal. He went to each kennel gate, calling out to each dog, and then going to the gate carefully, commanding them to step back as he walked inside to retrieve each feeding dish so that he could fill it with food.

Pointing to the kennels on the left side, Tony explained, "These dogs are the youngest ones. We will raise them up a bit more and then they will go up to be with my son in Kansas to be trained as hunting dogs."

I continued to see how calculated Tony's every move was as he filled the dishes, traced back to the dog pens and placed food in each of different kennels. He truly loved doing this for man's best friend, and though he may not show it too much on the outside, you know that he has a great affection for these animals.

Before we left the kennel area, he asked me to

come upstairs to see what he proudly called *"The Man Cave."*

Tony as he is training one of his bird dogs

He showed me around and then stated, "I kind of told Cheryl what I wanted out here 'cause I like to play dominoes, especially a game called forty-two."

He pointed to the left, "That old table there came out of the domino hall of Winnsboro and was there when I was a kid. It is about sixty years old."

Looking at the table it had obviously been recoated with glossy black paint, and it was placed just off to the left of the doorway for easy access.

Tony smiled and said, "We have meetings out here for the guys, and it gives us a place to go. If you look around you can see that this place is decorated with John Deer paraphernalia. I've spoken at many safety meetings for that company, and when I go, they usually give me something for '*the man cave*.'"

Tony then pointed to some old tin that bordered the room, and said, "I have had this for many years and I held on to it because I thought someday I was going to be able to use it. Cheryl said it would look great in here, and everyone else seems to agree that it unmistakably does."

I doted on the place myself seeing by the evidence that a lot of thought and love went into making this place comfortable and conveniently accessible for Tony. As I looked around at the large addition built separate from the house and near the dog kennels, it was easy to perceive that Tony was extraordinarily happy here. There was a couch and air conditioner. He mentioned that they were talking about getting a TV and some cable run out to the place so that he can listen to the ball games. Off the front of the room were some comfortable deck chairs and a cozy porch area just to sit and talk and look over the Crow Angus Farms. It was quite a site that morning as the sun was shining brightly over the lush green fields of trees and grassy meadows where wild flowers started to forge their way upward from the dusk of wintertime. Though it was officially still winter when I visited, the days were relatively warm and spring was undeniably in the air.

Rudy was still romping around very much like a young pup would with the other family dog named Punkin. Once Tony finished telling me about the man cave, we left out to go feed the cattle. Immediately, while Tony was at the top of the stairs, he called out to Rudy. Within seconds, Rudy took his rightful place next to his master and the working leash was placed back on him. Now, when the leash is on Rudy, he knows it is time to work. That is also an indication for all other observers to not pet Rudy when he is on the job.

Once Rudy was harnessed, he and Tony were off. Tony commanded to Rudy, "Take me to the gate

Rudy."

Rudy obediently followed every command without question or hesitation. His work is not only done flawlessly, but you could see that Rudy was ever so careful about the way he led Tony. As I followed the two of them down through the pasture and then to the barn, I could see the kindred spirit that had bonded them, as if it became almost tangible. Tony trusts Rudy with his life. Rudy has earned that respect through his unquestionable loyalty and obedience.

"Take me to the barn Rudy, Take me to the barn." Tony commanded.

As we arrived at the gate to the barn, Rudy had directed Tony to the side of the gate where it opens. Tony pointed that out to me and how imperative it was for Rudy not only to learn the gates, but to lead him to the part of the gate that opened.

I asked Tony, "How long did it take for Rudy to learn how to get around on the farm?"

Tony holding Rudy's leash, looked down at him and continued, "It took him about two months. Mind you, he had never had seen anything but the city, so this was all new to him. He was only familiar with cement buildings and sidewalks. Here he has an entire pasture of cattle grazing on the countryside, and a totally different lifestyle, but he has done well!"

After opening the gate, we entered the barn. Tony took his walking cane and reached down inside a barrel to check and see if what he expected might be there. As suspected, a raccoon was in the bottom of the barrel, and it could not get out. Tony could not sense my immediate apprehension about the situation.

Tony laughed, "I've been trying to get my helper to get rid of that thing once and for all, but all he does is let him out of the barrel, and so that little fellow returns regularly for a feeding of corn."

Tony slightly tilted the large barrel to show me the visitor, and to try to see if the raccoon would jump out, but it would not. This little raccoon was not so little, and I can tell you that this girl wasn't going to heed and lay the barrel down so the little critter could possibly retaliate. Tony, finally sensing my apprehension, though I never said a word, decided to leave well enough alone.

Once in the harness, Rudy knows it is time for work.

Tony filled up the bucket with food from another barrel, and headed out to feed his cattle as usual. He went about his business, walking to each separate pasture and asking Rudy to take him to each entry gate. I marveled at his ability and sense of direction out there on the farm. Rudy was astute and awaited every command, carefully and constantly keeping an eye on Tony. When Tony would drop the leash to do some work, Rudy would wander only a few feet away and keep looking back periodically checking on Tony, as if he was waiting for the next command.

I do have to mention that the cattle eyed me a lot, being that I was a stranger, and I was somewhat apprehensive about them because of their size, more than their demeanor.

Tony said, "Get up here by me, and don't worry. None of these cattle are going to hurt you. If I had one here that would, he wouldn't last long. I can't afford to be concerned about my safety while out on the farm."

The remaining time, I took him up on his offer as I walked beside, and not behind him and Rudy as we were out with the cattle. I looked over at Tony while we were walking, and he had an immense smile on his face. He was at home, and he loved being able to care for his livestock and have the freedom to do it independently, all because of Rudy. Likewise, Rudy seemed happier than ever when he was working. He thrived on helping Tony, and you could see it in his demeanor, as well. If you were to close your eyes and listen to Tony talk to Rudy, you would know instantly that they were best friends, and you may even wonder if Rudy is a dog or a human being. Rudy almost struts when he is given a command. It is a form of a challenge to him, I suppose, and he shines at what he does best; and that is keeping his master safe and away from all harm. What a joy to watch these two at work. What a privilege to meet not only Tony, but this remarkable creature that not only is Tony's Leader Dog, but in every aspect, part of the family.

CHAPTER SIX

Family Crisis

Later in the night while I was visiting the Crow Farms, we were sitting at the kitchen nook finishing dinner and just chatting. We had been gone most of the time as I was interviewing people, and Cheryl, Tony and I were a bit tired from a full day. During my stay, I had asked every question imaginable about the accident. I had talked to Tony, Tony's coworkers, close friends and family, and yet, there was one question I had not asked as of yet. To some it may seem formidable. However, to me, it was paramount and necessary to get to the bottom of the matter. I am sure by now, that you the reader have wondered about it too, and I could not let it slide. I had only one more day to obtain all of the information needed to get started on the project, and now was as an opportune time as any to make the inquiry. There was no need to put it off any longer. Finally, as we sat there in light conversation, I looked at Tony and continued, "Tony? I have heard a lot of extraordinary stories and have acquired some excellent insight for the book as of today, but what I would like to hear about is whether you ever struggled emotionally or spiritually with what has happened to you. You say that you had to be strong, and your friends and family have all concurred as to how strong you were and still are. Nevertheless, did you ever get upset about being shot, and did you ever have a moment of hopelessness come over you while thinking about your loss?"

Tony paused, and leaned back once again as if to contemplate my pointed inquisition. Then a mere smile appeared on his face. It was one of unrelenting purpose. Without missing a beat, he quietly breathed deep and started in. It was almost as if he knew the question would eventually be asked, and staying true to form, he was ready to take it on.

He leaned forward and looked at me, and if I did not know better, I would have thought he could actually see me. He was that intent on relaying the story accurately.

Clearly speaking he interjected, "I was at my lowest point just three months after the accident. My eye was hurting me, and I was tired of being sick, feeling bad, and being in pain. I had—had enough, when I just walked outside and looked straight up and screamed, 'God, why did you do this to me!!?'"

Cheryl found me weeping and suggested, "Maybe you need to talk to someone."

She was right, and I answered, "Call Brother James. I need to get him over here."

At that time, Brother James was his family's pastor and literally lived directly down the road from the Crow family. In just a few minutes he arrived, went outside to where Tony was seated, and both took off for a walk through the farm.

They had only been walking a few moments when Bro. James asked, "What's your problem Bud?"

"I am mad at God. He should not have done this to me and my family!" Tony blurted out.

Bro. James was not surprised at all when he saw

Tony's reaction. It was something he had expected to happen anytime, and he was already prepared to help Tony deal with it. "Let's go for a drive."

At that time, Tony had much trouble riding in a vehicle. He would become acutely nauseated and often overcome with motion sickness shortly after being blinded. Tony would request the driver to turn off to the side of the road just so he could vomit, when riding in a car. It was no obstacle to Bro. James as Tony warned him. He just insisted they needed to go, and as warned, Tony did get sick a few times on the road as they traveled to Sulphur Springs, TX.

After arriving in Sulphur Springs, they purchased some feed for the cattle and then went to Braum's Ice Cream Store for a milk shake. Tony knew that he most likely would get sick from it, but he got it anyway.

Suddenly Bro. James came out with, "You're Job man! You're Job in the bible. It took something dramatic to get your attention because you and Job are natured the same way. It took something like this to rattle your chain and get your attention."

He quoted some verses and then said, "Job yelled at God. He actually lashed out at God and asked, "Why did you do me like this?"

He went on to say, "It took that to get Jobs attention. There is nothing wrong with being angry at God, because that is our human nature. God says, 'I made him mad and I got his attention! Well, He has finally gotten your attention, hasn't He?'"

Tony knows now that God did not *do* this to him, but that God allowed the accident to happen to him.

Tony thought all about what Bro. James had said, and they talked out a lot more of the issues on the way back. Tony got sick three or four more times on the way back to the farm.

Bro. James would come out on the side of the truck with Tony and mention, "That's it man!! Get rid of it! Maybe it's not actually the milk shake you're throwing up. Maybe it is just—everything."

They arrived home after talking and talking about the problem and Tony could not contain his suffering any longer as he began once again to weep. Bro. James wept with him and then reminded Tony, "I have something that I want to tell you. Remember when you went in for that last surgery and we came over with twenty people to pray for you?"

Recalling that night, Tony answered, "Yes."

"Well ever since that time when we prayed and had hopes that God would restore your eyesight, and it did not work, I got mad at God too. I quit driving by your house because I was so mad at God for not restoring your vision. I would say, 'God he deserves to see.'"

As they sat there, Bro. James continued, "I have been struggling since I laid hands on you and prayed for you that night for God to restore your sight, and you had surgery the next day, and it didn't work. Now you have helped me, and I have helped you, and we can go on with our lives."

Tony concluded that together they both got it out of their systems and he realized how powerful that moment was for both of them.

In 2012, at the time I flew in to visit with the Crow family, their daughter Candace Crow was preparing to fly out to do ministry in Africa. We decided to rendezvous in Dallas, and spend some time together so that I could hear her side of the story, before I left for Winnsboro the next morning.

I had actually spent time with Candace and her mother a few months prior as we had all gone to Israel together. I was impressed by her sweet spirit and willingness to serve with a compassion for other people. We went to a local diner and then ended up back at the hotel for the interview.

I asked Candace a plethora of questions, and she willingly answered most of them. Candace remembers her childhood as a wonderful time in her life. She stressed how her parents were always there for her and her brother Landon. They were present at ball games and other events that they were involved in.

She added, "My dad worked shift work, but when he wasn't working, he was always there."

As a fifth grader, Candace's mom went on disability/ retirement due to a chronic lung disease. Regardless, she was always available to take Candace where she needed to be and to spend countless hours doing the normal activities that mom and daughters usually do.

As far back as she can remember her family was always in church. Though they attended church, she agreed that they did not talk much about the Lord at home.

Candace added, "We did not have family times where we would read the bible or pray together, but we had a very loving home. I have never heard my parents argue; in fact, I never heard them fight, ever."

She remembered summer times in the Crow home and that usually meant family vacations every summer to a different place. They traveled all over the United States and would also go skiing every year. The Crow home was more like the community gathering place for friends, especially Candace's and Landon's as they had a pool and plenty of room for everyone to come and have an enjoyable time.

Candace has fond memories of her grandparents on her Dad's side. "I grew up with my grandparents living next door to us. They were always a part of our lives. Our family lived in the same house the entire time that I grew up, so security was a given for me. Landon and I were the only grandchildren, so a lot of the events and parties revolved around us. My childhood was full of fun and lots of love." Candace's grandparents on Cheryl's side of the family lived in Winnsboro and they were always around. All the holidays were spent together with both sets of grandparents.

Candace's fondest memories of her father Tony would be the times they were together in the truck going somewhere. "We always could talk about anything, and dad was always so supportive of me.

Skiing was another sport that always brought us closer, but honestly, we grew much closer after the accident. We talk a lot more than we ever have before. Of course, talking is my dad's main channel now for communication. We have found a more common ground as dad's relationship with God is much different now than when I was growing up. What I am trying to say is that he always knew the Lord, but dad depends on God now, for everything."

Candace Crow, founder of Called Ministries.

Crow Family from left to right: Landon, Julie, Tony, Baby Macy, Cheryl and Candace

Growing up it was always easier for Candace to talk to her mom, and for Landon to talk to his dad. Landon and Tony shared the same passion for hunting and Candace and Cheryl shared the same passion for mission work, and that lent to them spending more time together. Candace admits that before the accident, it was always easier to talk to her mom, but things are changing now.

When the accident occurred, Candace was a junior in college at Dallas Baptist University. I had not planned on being home at the time of the tragedy, as my boyfriend and I were going to spend Valentine's Day together, but he unexpectedly got called in to work, so I came home to be with my family. Candace concludes, "I decided to drive home that night, and let me tell you, I never had done that. I never drove home at eleven 'o clock at night. That was way out of the norm for me."

When she came home, she realized that her dad and her brother had gone to West Texas to go hunting. The next day she went to see some friends in town. While she was visiting her friends, the call came in that her dad had been shot, and there were no other details. She panicked and drove home immediately. Upon arrival, Candace and Cheryl and Cheryl's parents drove to Dallas to meet Tony at Parkland Hospital.

While they were driving, they began to talk about Landon and her dad. They had no report as to how the accident had actually occurred but before receiving an update, they actually said that they hoped Landon was not involved in it. They knew it would cause some ripple effects if that were the case. On the drive to the hospital, their hopes were crushed when they heard that Landon accidentally shot Tony. All that they could think of was how difficult it was going to be for Landon to overcome such a tragedy.

When I asked the following question of Candace during the interview she visibly froze, momentarily. She debated as to whether she should say what she wanted to say but after some coaching from me, she became transparent and revealed what disturbed her the most.

I posed, "Candace, how did you react to the

accident?"

She braced herself emotionally and admitted, "Personally, I do not know if I want my dad to know this, because I was closer with my mom, and if I had to lose a parent, I would hope it would not be my mom. I felt so guilty feeling that way, and we did not know how serious the shooting was at that time. I told the Lord how sorry I was that I ever felt that way, and I can't believe that I would even think of choosing one parent over another. However, when emotions run deep, as they do in times of tragedy, no one knows how they are going to feel about things, or react to it. I just had to give that to the Lord."

Prior to the accident, Candace remembers her dad as a highly independent person, often known as a "man's man." He was capable of doing most things on his own, and he was always adept at accomplishing anything he put his mind to. By the world's standards, he would not be considered educated, but her dad is exceptionally intelligent and capable of doing anything he puts his mind to. Unfortunately, he would tell you that too. Her dad had a sense of arrogance about him, but after the accident, it was particularly evident to Candace that he had changed.

Remembering recent days after the accident, Candace continued, "After the accident, the burden of responsibility fell on my mom, and her life changed as drastically as dad's in a lot of ways. They used to share responsibilities, but now she carries the majority of things. Dad helps around the house with things that he can do, like dishes and laundry. I know that mom appreciates that. At first she had all the responsibilities of the farm, feeding animals and caring for the hunting dogs and all that. It was a huge load, but she did it. It could have been easy for my mom to say *"This is too hard,"* and runaway or shut down, and I am sure that she might have thought about it at one time or another. However, she has done amazingly well with everything!"

Candace recalled, "Dad could have reacted in the same way, but he kept moving forward too, and I am proud of both of them and what they have accomplished through this time in their lives," she smiled. She realizes that Landon knows that it was a fluke, crazy accident, but she is convinced that he still feels guilty, regardless.

Candace seemingly gathering her thoughts, then carried on, "No one has ever blamed Landon for this, nor would any of us ever want to be in his shoes. You see, Landon is remarkably like dad, independent. With that being said, he does not share his feelings very much, and I think that he bottles them up inside of himself at times."

Out of the four in their immediate family, Candace stated that she is most likely the one less affected by the accident. It did affect her, but, not to the extremes that it affected her dad, her mom or her brother. My goals for life remained the same, and that was to travel as a missionary. My parents are a critical part of that, as God has used them to provide those opportunities for me.

"Candace, what has it been like for you now knowing that your dad is somewhat of a celebrity?" I asked.

"I heard my dad speak for the first time in 2011. Through the years, people have come up to me and said, 'Your dad just touched my life, he is really good! What he says is just so incredible!' What I think about when they say things like that is; my dad is *just* my dad. He is a good ole country boy. He is not a polished, professional speaker. I genuinely thought people were just being polite. Later on when I finally heard him speak at a safety conference in Louisiana, I was taken aback. Dad, mom and I were walking around the conference room before his time to speak, and dad would tease me about his celebrity status. It became a joke in the family. But while we were walking around a person ran up to us and said, 'Oh—You're Tony Crow!'"

"Later on when he spoke, there were a few times that I became acutely emotional. I began to see what others were seeing in my dad. Dad is GOOD, and he is exceptionally talented at what he does! He engages people, because he is an extraordinary story teller. It is remarkable for me to see how far he has come as a speaker."

Reflecting on her dad, Candace said, "Dad spends much more time out at the dog pens with is dogs. When he is wrestling with life matters, he goes out to his place called the *man cave*, and he spends time in prayer. I do not know how many hours daddy spends down there talking to the Lord. I know that everything changed after the accident and that his prayer life has increased. I have witnessed him and realize now that he is more humble and more patient in areas of his life. He not only has had to rely on others differently than ever before, he is learning on how to rely on God differently, as well."

The final person that I was anxious to interview was Cheryl Crow. In my four days with this family, I had learned that she was a woman who wore many hats. Perhaps that is not so unusual for the woman of the household, but after watching her cook, taxi, run the business, calendar events, care for Tony, and on and on, I began to wonder if she was actually "Wonder Woman" in disguise.

As we sat to talk about her side of the accident, and how it has changed her life forever, she immediately began to dote on Tony, and how he can do so much, even being blind. She said that he was responsible for coming up with the plans to renovate the kitchen, which would begin in a week after my stay with them.

Cheryl says, "Tony can visualize things in his mind, and since he has such a clear memory, it actually works to his credit when it comes to things like this."

I asked, "Cheryl, when did you meet Tony?"

She smiled and sat back as she reflected, "I met Tony in the first grade, and we were in the same class together. We knew each other all through school, and started dating as juniors in high school. We actually broke up when I went on to college, and then got back together during my last semester. We married on June 3, 1978 and have been married for almost thirty-four years now."

I wanted to know Cheryl's perspective about the accident, and how Tony was prior and afterward. As his life mate, she probably has seen the transformation in Tony more than anyone else, and I thought it was vital to get her input.

According to Cheryl, prior to the accident, Tony was always independent, and that would upset her, as he would go out hunting in Knox City by himself. It would concern her so much, as she could not imagine why Tony would want to go out hunting by himself. She realized early in their relationship that Tony has never had to have people around him, and now she believes that is one factor that has truly helped him through his blindness.

Cheryl proudly stated, "He has always been a devoted father and husband, and hard worker."

On that particular day of the accident, Cheryl was at home, when she received the call from some of Tony's friends in West Texas. They did not give her any details but only insisted that she needed to get to Dallas. After she contacted Candace to inform her, they both left on the two hour drive as soon as possible. On the way up, Candace and other people started calling everyone that they knew, and the word spread quickly about the shooting.

Cheryl explained, "At that time, I had no details, nor did I know that Landon was the one who had accidentally shot Tony. I only knew that Tony had been shot. I actually think that I was in shock, and remained in shock the whole time that he was in the hospital. I suspect this because honestly, I just had no emotions; I couldn't even cry. I also have blocked things out to the point that I cannot remember a lot about the time of the accident. What I do remember is that there were a lot people there at Parkland Hospital in Dallas. These were people that we knew, and they had come to the hospital to check on Tony, as well as support us as a family. There was seventy-two people there that all consisted of Landon's friends, Candace's friends, and our friends.

Over the next day or two, people kept coming in

to see us and Tony. Our pastor stayed until four o' clock Sunday morning and then he had to go back and preach a sermon that same Sunday. It was phenomenal to see all of the support that we were receiving."

When I asked Cheryl how this accident changed her life, her initial reaction was laughter and then she almost shouted, "It completely changed it!"

She went on to describe how she immediately became a caregiver. "I am so fortunate that Tony does as much as he does. I truly am. As a caregiver, I have had to learn a lot of things about the farm, mainly because Tony still wanted to keep his identity, and the farm has always been a part of him."

Cheryl continued to say how she had to learn how to operate the tractor, put hay out for the cattle, and learn how to do all the farm care. She was never involved in that until the accident happened, so she was on a momentous learning curve, not only learning how to care for the animals, but for her husband in a different way. She was remarkably candid about how unhappy that she was due to the extra work load. Afterward, she would be overcome with guilt, because she was grateful that Tony was still alive, though he was blind.

Cheryl insisted, "There is one thing that I want to emphasize, and that is how much an accident like this impacts the entire family, especially the spouse. This might not be necessarily true if it were reversed, because the man is usually the caregiver. Now I have had to take up that position for the largest part, and I am extremely grateful for what Tony can do. God has helped me all the way through it."

Cheryl went on to share something that every reader needs to know and comprehend. Smiling, she pointedly explained, "You know, I actually received a miracle from God. I had chronic asthma. Actually, it was so severe, that I was forced to take disability retirement from teaching. The entire time that I taught school, which was for thirteen years, I was in and out of the hospital constantly, and had an atomizer with me at all times. I was on steroids for seventeen years. When the doctors here could do no more for me, they sent me to the Mayo Clinic. After arriving, they gave me the whole report that my lungs were barely breathing. The doctors here told me that it would take two years to get me off steroids. Well, God knew how much work that needed to be done on this farm after the accident, and so He took it away from me. I mean, it is a miracle, and I know it is a miracle!"

As I listened to Cheryl talk about the healing miracle in her life, I remembered how so many people had prayed for Tony to be healed, and it never came to pass. I thought it all out and sensed that maybe it did not happen the way people expected. Tony was not physically healed, but nevertheless, Tony was healed spiritually and emotionally. God in his unique purpose for Tony found a way to make him totally dependent on the Lord. I believe Cheryl was healed physically, so that she could take care of Tony.

Cheryl continued telling me about her condition prior to the miracle. She had incredible difficulty just walking from the kitchen to the barn without struggling to breathe. Tony's accident was in

February and in May, or early June, she was completely off of the steroids that her body had become totally dependent upon just to breathe. She is fully off all asthma medication and has not had one issue with it since the apparent miracle of healing in her life. People who have known her for a lifetime cannot believe that she has been set free from her breathing issues. This was primarily due to the fact that Cheryl was one of the most affected asthma people in town and that she almost died from it. She understands thoroughly how God intervened, so that she could provide Tony the care he needs, and so they both could function as normal as possible.

I could not refrain from asking, "Cheryl, what do you believe prepared you in life when it comes to caring for Tony now?" Hands down, she admitted that having a relationship with God prepared her the very most. She is a bit of an optimist, much like Tony, believing that everything that happens to us happens for a reason.

After the accident, she put herself in Tony's shoes, by simply observing what it would be like if the situation was turned around. She spent a long time imagining what she would need. During those months, she entirely lost her appetite, and with it, 40-50 pounds. This is how her body absorbed the trauma.

She will be the first to comment, "Trauma may not affect you until six months or so later."

Further down the road of dealing with trauma, she was hospitalized because she could not eat. Her thoughts could have been labeled somewhat depressive as she worried about herself, and if anything happened to her, that there would be no one to care for Tony. She spent an enormous amount of time planning things for Tony so he would have something to do. Eventually she learned that Tony was just fine being by himself. Personally, she insists that would never work for her, because she is such a people person. Regardless, Tony is content sitting out on the porch, as much as being in a crowd of people. Tony loves people, but his comfort level doesn't depend on socializing. He is extremely comfortable in his own skin, and according to Cheryl, he always has been.

"How did you ever come to the conclusion that you could leave Tony for a few hours by himself, and not feel guilty about it?" I queried.

'Well, it took me a long time to get to that point, to actually leaving him here alone without worrying that something dreadful would happen to him. I am so grateful that God finally gave me a peace about all of it, and now it does not bother me in the least to be gone all day, knowing that Tony is here alone. He is comfortable with it too, and that sincerely is an enormous help."

Cheryl never pretends that the transition was easy, and confessed that the first six months to a year were harder than anyone could ever imagine. Tony would become frustrated, and Cheryl would follow suit. It was most difficult and enormously challenging learning how to care for a blind person.

Cheryl added, "For instance, you cannot leave a door partially opened, because Tony simply cannot see it, and he will run right into it. You can't leave a cabinet door half open, and you have to shut up everything. One of the hardest things that I had to learn was to be more organized. I am not a well-organized person, and a blind person can only function well in an organized environment. In other words, Tony cannot be going around hunting for things."

I sat and thought how two other people had told me about the following incident and Cheryl would make the third. Of course, this episode is pretty *way out there*, even for most of us. One day, on the farm, they experienced a water leak and were forced to turn off the water. Back then Landon was home, and he was looking all over for the hack saw so that he could cut the pipe off and replace it. Cheryl joined in the hunt at no avail. Tony kept telling both of them where it was, but neither of them could locate it. Out of frustration, she and Landon hopped in the truck and went to town to get one. Before they got back, Tony, being blind, had gone into the shop area, and after briefly patting around with his hands he found the hack saw, right in clear sight. He went out and had the pipe fixed before they ever returned.

Standing corrected, people often assume what a blind person can, and cannot do. All of those who know Tony are also aware of the fact that he sets no real limits on the things that he can accomplish. The general consensus from family and friends is that God made Tony with an independent nature, knowing full well that the day would come that he would be blinded. That same nature has assisted him immensely in and through his sightlessness and given him the courage to carry on.

Now that the Crow's travel all over the states for Tony's speaking engagements, they have admitted that they learn about tragic stories and how people say they never would have gotten past such a tragedy.

Cheryl smiled, "I am so blessed that Tony has gotten past it and that he feels comfortable with doing things and getting out in the world. So many people that experience like tragedy's wind up just sitting on a couch the rest of their lives. He is such a visionary with a keen sense of memory and that obviously helps him in seeing things in his mind's eye. For instance, after we had the new rock facade put on our house last year, some people came from across the street for a visit. The lady said, 'Oh Tony, I wish that you could see it, it looks so good! Tony did not miss a beat in replying that he could see it and that he could essentially visualize it and grasp precisely what the house looks like now.'"

Cheryl shared that she had several people come out to the house and try to redesign the new kitchen, but Tony's design was the best one. He came up with a plan to knock a wall out, and put cabinets to the end of that wall. He figured out where to put the bar, etc. Not one of the experts came up with an idea as plausible as Tony's. His internal vision is his strong suit, and it has been so helpful for the entire family.

"One thing we do a lot of around here, is *laugh. We laugh* about his blindness," Cheryl giggled. "If you don't laugh you'll eventually cry, so we have a lot of humorous moments between us. Tony is a tremendous crack up anyway, so there is a lot of laughter in this place, after all, laughter is the best kind of medicine."

Cheryl candidly replied that everyone realizes that

Tony could have been instantly killed that day. If Landon would have been standing only 25 feet closer, there would be no need to be having this conversation, because there would be no Tony. The family motto is: "Never feel sorry for yourself; there is always someone else who has it lot worse than you do."

Cheryl struggled to say, "The hardest thing for me to think about was what we were going to do for the rest of our lives, since he had no job. It is unbelievable how God has opened up doors for us with all his speaking engagements. We are truly blessed."

Tony started speaking after people at work kept encouraging him to tell his story, as well as people at the church. Anyone who knew Tony back then, also knew that he never spoke in front of people, and Cheryl asked him one day, "If you could tell your story and save one family the grief that we have been through wouldn't it be worth it?"

His friends at work kept consistently encouraging him, and then God opened up the opportunity for him to speak at a big conference. He actually had two large conferences in that year, and then the business started taking off from that point onward. One thing that makes Tony so attractive to those who are looking for a speaker is that he comes from an ordinary background. Cheryl says that they are just like the people who sit in the audiences where he speaks. Tony worked at a hard job, and everyone who has ever seen him in action when it comes to speaking, is seriously impacted by his story. The Crows have never solicited for speaking engagements, as all of their business has come through word of mouth.

What this tragedy has done is given Tony a legitimate purpose for his life. He has so much to offer. Since the accident, the main thing that Cheryl has noticed about Tony is that he has become more caring and compassionate.

Tony is always telling people that it is necessary to know that we still have something to contribute in life. What he is doing is God's purpose in his life right now. His attitude towards this and everything else has helped immensely.

Cheryl agreed, "I truly believe that God has opened doors for us, and we are particularly thrilled to see Isaiah 42 come to pass in our lives.

"And I will lead the blind in a way that they do not know, in paths that they have not known I will guide them. I will turn the darkness before them into light, the rough places into level ground. These are the things I do, and I do not forsake them." (ESV) English Standard Version.

One thing about Tony Crow *now* versus when he had his sight, is the fact that he judges people without his eyes. For instance, a man had come to do some work for the Crows on their property. He was donning some long, straggly hair, a beard, and sporting tattoos all over his arms, but Tony hired him, because Tony could not see him to judge him. The man happened to work out perfect. The Crows tell people everywhere that we must learn not to judge people with our eyes. Tony gets irritated at people who talk about other people, and how they look. They have both confirmed that it does not matter to

God, because God sees the heart.

Until you encounter trials, you do not think of hardships and how they affect you in every area of your life. Cheryl says, "I tell people, 'You know it can be difficult at times. For instance, you try carrying two bags of luggage, a blind guy, and a seeing-eye dog while you run through an airport hoping to catch the next connection. It can be tremendously challenging!'"

The same rings true because of their intenerate travel, Tony is in and out of hotel rooms all of the time. Each time, he is forced to learn the layout of the room upon arrival. In addition, Cheryl says there is another big obstacle for them when they travel and that is the fact, when Tony has to go to the bathroom. Many places now have family or companion restrooms, and it works out great. However, it is very upsetting when we find that one person has used the companion restroom, leaving us to wait. When there is no companion restroom, Tony is forced to find his way around the restroom with the use of his cane. We are grateful that there have been so many nice people willing to help. There is a tremendous amount on his plate when they have to travel, but Tony has been a trooper about that. The Crows are well aware that in any kind of tragedy, that there are a lot of difficulties, but you can overcome them, as Tony is a perfect example of that.

At the end of his speaking engagements, Tony will open up the floor for any questions, and people have asked, "What is it going to be like when you have grandchildren?"

Tony knows that he will never get to see their faces. Tony wants people to understand that accidents change everything. He will answer folks and say, "I'm going to the best blind grandpa you will ever see!" He also knows that he will never see what Candace looks like when she walks down the aisle to get married.

Many times during his presentation, Cheryl will go out of the room, or sit in the back and do something else. At first, she cried every time he gave a presentation.

Cheryl conceded, "The one thing that I am so

thankful for is that Tony and Landon are still majorly close."

People will ask, "How were you able to get up and keep going on?"

Tony abruptly replies, "I did it for Landon"

Landon had a lot of guilt, even though this was not his fault. It is just like a car accident. If you are in a car accident, it may not have been your fault. Nevertheless, if you injured someone in the process, you may carry around that guilt for a lifetime. Tony knows that if he would have just lied around on the couch and never gotten up to do anything, that it would have compounded the guilt that Landon was experiencing at the time. Tony often tells the audience, "I had a driving force to get me up and keep me going and to go on with my life." He credits all of that to Landon.

One of the number one questions asked after Tony's presentation is, "How is your son doing?"

Cheryl answered, "We want people to know that Landon is doing well. He lives in Kansas and has been married for the past four years to his wonderful wife, Julie. What you may find odd, is what Landon is dong for a living now. He is a professional guide/kennel manager at a 5-star hunting resort in Kansas. He takes people quail and pheasant hunting every day from the beginning of October until the end of March. It is truly amazing that Landon went back to hunting and is doing the *very* thing that he and Tony love so much to do together. As you can well imagine, he is very conscious of safety as he takes clients into the field to hunt.

Tony still enjoys hunting also. Several years ago he was able to start hunting again as a friend of his put a laser on the bottom of Tony's deer rifle.

**Tony and Landon on their first pheasant hunt
since Tony was blinded**

Someone might ask, 'How does this help a blind man since he can't see the laser dot?"

The fact is that Tony has someone sitting in the deer stand with him, and with their assistance they will tell Tony to move his rifle to the right or left, or up and down and when he can shoot.

Since then, he has been able to kill two deer and a wild hog. In March of 2012, Tony was able to put the shotgun in his hand for the first time since the accident, and Landon guided him on a quail and pheasant hunt. Tony was able to locate the quail and pheasant just by sound. His next challenge will be to try and kill a turkey in the wild.

Our daughter Candace finished college at DBU and then joined the staff at our church—FBC of Winnsboro, where she served for five years as Interim Youth and Missions Outreach Director. She felt the Lord call her to resign and devote her time to full-time missions. She now has a ministry called, "Called Ministry" that she founded. She currently takes people all over the world to share the Good News about Jesus Christ.

Another frequent question posed to Tony after he speaks is, "What do you miss the most because of your blindness?"

The answer Tony gives sometimes shocks people. He says, "I miss driving." He knows people think that he should say, seeing the beautiful countryside, as we travel, and especially the faces of his family, and he does miss that very much, though his answer is always driving. Of course, Tony has to always add in his humor and say, "If you had to ride with my wife in a metroplex (for example NYC or Chicago, etc.,) you would want to drive TOO!" He then adds, "It's nice sometimes to be blind—you don't see those near misses!!!"

His answer is always "driving" as it represents his independence that he lost to blindness. He does not have the capability of going anywhere he wants to, anytime he wants to go. He tells attendees that he would love to just go get in the car and drive home.

As for Candace and Landon, they both have dealt with this issue in a great way. Landon has never seen Tony's presentation. They just do not talk about it much though Landon seems to be doing fine. There may be a time later on when he has children and so, but he seems to be doing exceptionally well at this time.

Landon Crow

Cheryl remembered, "During Landon's senior year in high school, when Landon was getting a little testy with me, I asked, "What's the matter?" My thoughts were that he was experiencing awful dreams or something like that, but Landon started crying and confessed, *'You'll never know mom, you weren't the one who pulled the trigger.'*

You know, he has to carry that with him forever, but life has to go on, and I am so very proud that he is doing what he is doing now. Tony makes sure that people know what Landon is doing for a living. He is doing the one thing that most people would never have thought he could do, and it is proof that God is healing him. He is working in Kansas as a hunting guide and the kennel manager of a 5—Star hunting resort, and we couldn't be more proud of him."

One matter that the Crows never thought about having to deal with as they travel and Tony speaks, are the people who might be totally against hunting. Someone, who was probably against hunting sent them the ugliest email and said, "How could you continue to trap and kill defenseless animals?"

Cheryl was remarkably sincere when she sent the woman a reply saying, "I am truly sorry that you are offended that Tony still wants to hunt. I appreciate your perspective, but I hope that you understand the significance of his presentation is that you have to get past tragedy. Tony will always enjoy hunting. We are aware that it wasn't the gun or hunting that caused the accident, it was the lack of safety practices."

She returned Cheryl's email reciting a single

word, "Karma."

The Crows understand that there are people who are against hunting, but those who focus on that and fail to understand the true meaning of Tony's goal in life, miss out on the story completely. Tony has had the courage, and determination to face the exact thing that took his eyesight away. Anyone who sees him today should know that they too can overcome any obstacle set before them. Tony is often asked what he does as a hobby, and he tells people with all sincerity that he still likes to hunt.

Tony was interviewed by Channel 7 News, the biggest television station in Tyler, Texas. They heard about Rudy, and they watched Rudy do what he does with Tony.

Cheryl was watching television one day, and they asked "Do you believe in stem cell research?"

In response to that question, she wrote in and replied, "Yes we do!" We do not believe in taking stem cells from aborted babies, but there are other stem cells available. The result is that Channel 7 came to the ranch to interview the Crows at their home. Tony made it abundantly clear that people understood that he was *not talking about abortion* stem cell research, but other means as it would be the only way that Tony might be able to see again if they are able to regenerate the one nerve of the eye that Tony still has.

Everyone in Winnsboro watches Channel 7 News. After that interview, the Crows received a nasty, unsigned email that was simply dreadful. It was essentially hate mail saying, "How can you even say that you believe in stem cell research and you call yourself a Christian!" It truly upset Cheryl, but then she thought to herself, "Until you have walked in the shoes of someone else, until you have known that this might be the only hope for someone to see, you don't understand it." Cheryl stayed upset about that email for quite a while.

In just a few moments, Cheryl changed the subject abruptly to tell me one thing that makes her laugh about Tony. She continued, "Tony tells this story about these guys who walk around and say they are so tough that they have gotten tattoos everywhere, etc. Tony will say, 'Well, I got a tattoo on my eye.' In reply, those same guys will respond, "Man! You truly are bad!'"

Cheryl concludes, "Tony has our Crow Farms cattle brand and the scripture Philippians 4:13 on his prosthetic eye. His other eye looks pretty bad because it is intrinsically dead. That is one reason why "we" wear sunglasses. A lot of blind people do not wear sunglasses, because a lot of people just lose their sight naturally, and it does not affect the aesthetics of their eyes. However, the accident makes Tony's eyes look bad, so he feels more confident wearing sunglasses.

I noticed when Cheryl was speaking that she used a considerable amount of "we'" in places like, ". . . *eye looks pretty bad because it is intrinsically dead. That is one reason why "we" wear sunglasses.*" At first I thought she was misspoken, but after hearing her talk about their story, I believe that they are so into this life together and that she is right by his side day and night. As his caregiver, she is also the one who does the scheduling for the business. They are inseparable at most times. I realized how valuable her statements were, when she would be talking about Tony and saying "we" instead of "he". I sensed this is one truly remarkable lady who takes her marriage vows seriously. When we marry, we become one, and she has done that more so than most marriage partners.

Tony credits his success to her, and God, so I know that he will not mind me saying that Cheryl is a strong woman who gracefully does the things that need to be done so that Tony can live as independently as possible. With her help, he is able to keep going, keep speaking, and sharing his compelling story with people everywhere.

Knowing what I know about Cheryl, I realize too that her faith has carried her through an enormous amount of fear, insecurity, and heartache and that most women might have never made it through such a crisis. Cheryl says that Tony is a trooper, but I think that Cheryl is a trooper too! That is what makes them such a dynamic duo. Once you meet them, you will agree with me, and all of their friends, that God has blessed them immensely in their relationship, and in every other area of life.

CHAPTER SEVEN

The Heart of Winnsboro

When I arrived in Winnsboro, I was taken back from its size, or should I say, lack of it. But what the town lacks in size, they make up with big hearted people. Every person that I met while visiting the farm, or while shopping through the market were warm and friendly, and if you could allow your mind to go back to a time in Mayberry, there were a lot of similarities. I mean, I never met Sheriff Andy, but I would not be surprised if the town sheriff possessed some of those qualities, as well. I was instantly enveloped into this small town of southern hospitality, to the point of almost a syrupy social atmosphere. I walked in a store, and noticed that a clerk was speaking compassionately to a man about his mama, and I thought she knew him personally. Later on, I realized that is just how folks are here. That clerk talked to everyone the same way with a smile and a genuine caring attitude. It was refreshing.

As I looked around at how most of the people were dressed, it immediately gave me a sense that these were hard working people; mostly ranchers, farmers and cattleman. The women were less driven to compete with each other by dressing up and donning jewelry and makeup, unless they were seen at church. But otherwise, they donned casual clothing and set the tone of the township by offering a smile and a "hello" to strangers. Men held doors open for other women and other men, and hospitality ran thick through the air of this quaint township. I am not saying that everyone here has that kind of attitude, but what I saw with my own eyes and witnessed as I spent an afternoon in town alone, well, allow me to say, that my perception isn't too far off. If I had found Aunt Bee, I might have been inclined to have packed up my things and moved here too.

I asked Cheryl to please tell me what Winnsboro,

TX is truly like, and she did!

Without hesitation, Cheryl started, "Winnsboro is a great town to raise a family. People know everybody and are supportive of everyone else. Of course, there is always a downside to that, and it is that everyone knows everyone else's business. Nevertheless, it has been a wonderful town to grow up in. Our kids were born and raised here, and we have been here our whole, entire lives."

When Tony was at the hospital after the accident, the nurse made a particularly valuable observation that resonates with the Crow's to this day. She informed them that they most likely would not have had the type of support shown them, if they had been from a big town. After Tony's accident, the Crow family was especially blessed by the hospitality and extraordinary effort put forth by the community. They did not have to cook meals for five entire weeks as prepared meals kept being delivered from church family, friends and community members on a daily basis. That, in itself, is a sign of the huge support that the Crow family received from folks in Winnsboro.

Part of that enthusiastic support came from the fact that Cheryl was a teacher here and that Tony grew up in that town, so most of the folks know them well. Tony's mother was also an Avon lady, so the "Crow" family roots run deep in Winnsboro, TX.

What you are about to read is an account of personal stories straight from the lives of some people in Winnsboro. These are not just any people, but these are the folks that Tony values as friends and coworkers and when it is all summed up, they are the very fabric and heartbeat of this community as a whole. In each of their lives, you will see a common thread running through their stories and character that cannot be mistaken as anything but deep appreciation and gratitude towards Tony. As mentioned earlier, the friends that Tony has are basically lifetime friends. Would I say that they are Winnsboro's finest? Well, I did not meet everyone who lived here, but I think you will agree with Tony, they are the cream of the crop. Because they are a tight knit group of friends that live in a tight knit community, I will let them share their own experiences with Tony prior and after the accident to this day.

I sat in the home of Donny and Phyllis Stone as they shared their own take on how they came to know Tony and what his life has personally meant to them. Phyllis has known Tony as long as she could remember.

"He is four years older than me." She smiled. Before the accident, Tony was always so competitive in playing dominoes, softball or whatever he was doing, and he has always been a lot of fun."

The day of the accident, the Stone couple was in Waco, TX at a Baylor game, when they received the phone call about Tony's accident. There was very little information given as they were simply told that Tony had been shot. Devastated by the news they left immediately to head for Dallas where he had been taken. When they finally arrived, Tony's family was there along with a magnitude of friends in Winnsboro. Tony and Cheryl lived two hours away from Dallas, but that did not stop their friends or church family from driving to Dallas to attend and to help them through this time. The Stone's relayed that it was truly touching, and a bit overwhelming to see so many people at the hospital.

As they arrived, they kept praying and asking God to help Tony. It turned out to be an extremely, scary ordeal as Tony continued to have blood draining from the sides of his eyes, and none of us knew for sure if he was ever going to be able to see again. Though Tony was conscious, he was experiencing a tremendous amount of pain.

Donny and Phyllis had been close friends with the Crow's prior to the accident, and they admittedly informed me that their relationship has even grown closer since the accident. They believe that it is mainly due to the fact that they speak to each other more often and pray for the Crow's more than they used to.

They also used to go snow skiing with Tony and Cheryl, and Phyllis added, "We still like to play dominoes, and we still like beating the *snot out of them* when we play."

Donny interjected that he has known Tony since 1971. "Tony and I played softball together when I was in seventh grade. After we became adults, our friendship remained. Phyllis and I usually go out to eat with Cheryl and Tony. Whenever there was a group fellowship from the church, it was either at their house, or our house. Our two homes were the main two gathering places for most of the church fellowships."

Donny admitted that he was in shock when he first heard about the accident. Upon arrival to the hospital they found it in chaos.

Donny explained, "I have actually worked in Parkland Hospital Emergency Room, and it is utter chaos there most of the time. When we arrived it literally looked like a total mass of confusion. There were so many patients there. They had patients in the hallway, because there were not enough rooms for all the patients that go to that hospital. There was another gunshot victim lying in the hallway when we arrived. This is not only the county hospital, but it is also one of the best trauma hospitals in the country, which is why Tony was taken there. Most of the people, who come in to the ER, probably have no friends or family with them. They initially get there on their own, and then leave alone. I say all this to say, when we saw the mass of people who came to see Tony, it was hard not to take notice of that. They actually set up a private room for all of us to wait inside and to gather together."

Donny said that the biggest change since the accident that he has seen in Tony is his ability to talk to people. "Prior to the accident, he would not sit here and talk in front of five people. Afterward, he is standing in front of thousands; I believe it has been a key factor in his emotional and mental healing. God has used this incident in his life to make him a viable witness, because he would have never gotten up to speak in front of anybody before the accident. My admiration for Tony is out of this world. There has always been an ardent friendship there, but my admiration is in how he unbelievably has handled the issue. I am amazed at how he was able to rationalize everything when the accident happened. His thought has never been on himself, it has always been on his son Landon. I know Tony has had to have moments of depression or self—pity, but *none of us* has ever seen it."

When Tony was first asked to speak at church, he refused. It was actually Donny who told him that he needed to tell his story. Tony insisted if he was going to speak that it would be at night, when less people attended.

Donny laughed, "Tony—you're blind! You don't know how many people are going to be there, so what difference does that make?"

Donny and Phyllis both feel very fortunate to this day, to have the Crow's in their life.

During the process of writing this book, I had the opportunity to speak with Dr. Brent Wadle, and his memory of the event was extraordinarily vivid. I asked him, "Did you actually drive to Parkland Hospital to see Tony? What was your first response when you saw him?"

"Yes. We received the call, and I was asked by the family to come up to Parkland Hospital to assess Tony. I was the family doctor at the time. When I saw Tony it was pretty scary, even though I was a physician. I've seen a lot of traumas in my life and emergency issues before. Tony had pellet holes all over his face and arms, just everywhere. It was pretty scary."

"Did you ever think that he would regain his eyesight?" I posed.

There was a long pause before answering, "No, I did not after seeing the extended damage to his eyes. I knew it would take a miracle from God if he were to regain his sight."

Again I continued, "Did your relationship change with Tony after his accident and did you witness any notable changes in Tony afterward?"

There was a brief silence once again, and then Dr. Wadle continued, "Tony was the type of guy that everyone liked. He was sure of himself, outgoing, sure of his abilities and plainspoken. He raised cattle and such and he was very down to earth, and he would do anything for you. His daughter Candace would babysit my kids and come over to our house and hang a lot with us, so we knew each other pretty well. I was the family doctor, and we remained good friends, the same as before. Tony's demeanor changed a lot. He had become a lot more humble and a lot more loving. Tony is a great guy with an attitude willing to do anything for you. Now he had to rely on others when his entire life was pretty much autonomous, not relying on anyone. I realized he was more sensitive and that God undoubtedly changed him through that accident and made him into what he is today. Since my move three years ago to Tyler, TX, I do not see the family as I used to."

Prior to that evening, I had the opportunity to meet Debbie and Benny Cowser. We sat at the kitchen bar and she started right in, "I have known Tony his entire life. Tony is about five years younger than I am, and I was like an older sister to both Tony and his best friend John Greer. I was also the one who always told them that they needed to go home and stay out of trouble. I remembered mostly when Tony was young that he was a baseball player. He was one of the best ballplayers you would have ever seen. I have never seen anyone throw a ball from center field to home plate like Tony does. So we would go out and watch the ball games, and it was like having two little brothers with me."

Debbie recalled, "Initially, when they received the call about Tony being shot, I thought that he had died, as there was no other information given. Thankfully, the party on the phone said, 'No, he's alive, but he has been critically shot.' They continued to keep us informed with updates."

Debbie says that Tony is the same guy he was prior to the accident. She smiled, "I have never heard Tony say a discouraging word about the accident; he has always been real upbeat. The only time I have seen him breakdown at all, is when I went to visit him in the hospital. He was able to manage pretty well with his emotions, until I arrived. Tony is one of these people who would say, 'Don't tell me that I can't do something, because I am going to show you that I can.' He has always been that way. Since the accident, he is that way—all the more! Tony's outlook on life has certainly inspired many."

Debbie remembered a remark that Tony made one day, "This is just a hurdle, and we are going to get through this." At first, Debbie believed that he was staying upbeat because of Landon, but later on she realized, that's just how Tony is.

Debbie continued, "For instance, Tony was an exceptionally good forty-two player, and we used to play it quite often. After the accident, Tony said that he wanted to play forty-two. I wandered how in the world he was going to do that being blind, but we got dominoes with braille, and he was able to play. It hasn't done much for our ego, because Tony still beats us—blind!"

She carried on, "If you know Tony, he has always loved baseball. When he was a kid you could see him throw a rock up in the air and when it fell from the sky, he would hit it with his bat. After he became blind, he wanted to try and hit a baseball again. So we went to the ball park to see if he could throw a ball up without sight, as he had done so many times before. It was amazing how he could figure out when the ball was going to be ready for a hit. He practiced for just a few minutes, and he was able to hit that ball just like before! He is simply amazing!"

Benny has known Tony for about forty years and he recalled the first time that they met. "I met him when I was a RA leader at church and he started participating in the group. We have a seven to eight year age variance between us, but we both like to hunt, and we always would go frog gigging and hunting together. On the day of the accident, if I remember right, I was at work, and one my friends called me and told me that there had been an accident and that Tony had been shot. We did not know the extent of the accident. Honestly, when I heard about it, I took it pretty hard. They told us that they had flown him to Abilene, and we waited and learned that he had been taken to Parkland Hospital in Dallas. John Greer and I left early that next morning to see him."

Benny stated that his and Tony's relationship has pretty much stayed the same since the accident, if not better. They do not get to spend as much time together, but they do, on occasion, still go hunting.

After that visit we went on to the restaurant I told you about earlier in Tony's story. A week later, I spoke with Roy Glynn Crow on the phone, because he does not live in Winnsboro. Roy chuckled, "As Tony's older brother, I thought him to be a pest. He was always following me around. It was a typical older brother and little brother relationship. We fussed and argued a lot like most siblings do, but we were extremely close friends. Needless to say, as we got older, and I was in college, and he was in high school that our relationship matured. We were closer back then. When he was young, I would have to say that our parents were a lot stricter on me than they were on him. For instance, I had come in from college one time and I was doing something on Saturday night. My mom said, 'Well, you need to be home at a certain time.'

"Mind you, Tony was in high school, and he had no curfew. So that was radically different from my high school days. Tony thought that was downright funny, but I didn't.'"

Roy reminisced about how he and Tony hunted and fished together, and how they worked together on the family farm raising cows. Roy admitted that he took advantage of Tony many times, simply because Tony was younger. He would pawn off harder and dirty jobs on Tony and he would drive the farm equipment and truck since he was the older one.

Roy's perspective was interesting as he stated that when Tony was young, that he was a bit mouthy. He remembered, "I played football, and I was a lot bigger than Tony back then and I still am. When I would come in to the parking lot there in Winnsboro, I looked over one time and Tony was there talking to some other guys. It appeared that he was engaged in a confrontation. So, I went to see what was going on, predicting that Tony had probably started it, and he had. He was mouthing off at those boys, and he was about to get in a fight."

Roy continued, "I stepped out of the truck and Tony saw me and said, 'Hey, my big brother is here, and we'll just take you all on—come on—we'll take you all on!!'"

Roy said, "Since it was just me and Tony and those four other guys, I asked them what exactly was going on."

Their reply was, "We don't have a problem with you, we just got a problem with him" as they pointed in Tony's direction.

Roy piped up, "If you got a problem with him, then you got a problem with me, because I am his brother."

After they decide to leave, Roy turned to Tony and said, "If you ever do that to me again, I am going to make sure you get it."

Roy said that he and Tony, like typical brothers, got into squabbles. Roy was very serious about his the sport of track, and one day he was running out at the track. Tony was playing around with some of his friends nearby.

Roy recalls, "Tony ran up behind me and tripped me, and I said, "Boy, you need to go on and leave me alone."

I turned and went off running again, and then he did it again. I guess he was showing off in front of his buddies. I got up, and I said, "I'm getting ready to tear into you.

"You think you are so big, come and get me!"

Tony shouted.

Well I did, and I smacked him right on the end of his nose, and broke it. I loaded him up in the car and took him home.

When we got home, my dad asked "What happened?"

Tony immediately cried, "He hit me!"

I then told my dad what happened and he said, "Boy—you are going to learn to keep your mouth shut."

Like most brothers at that age, that is how they were. As they grew up, time together became scarce. Time away from each other added to the distance between them.

Roy informed me that Tony was not real outgoing before the accident. He was especially reserved around people he had never met.

Roy admitted, "After the accident, he started traveling and speaking, and his whole personality towards people has changed. He is now one of the most outgoing people that you will ever meet, and he talks to anybody—anytime."

It was interesting hearing Roy's perspective. Siblings often can exaggerate things, as they remember them, but I sensed there was a lot of truth in what Roy Glynn had shared and it was obvious that he admires Tony for the man he is today.

One day, during my visit at the Crow Farms, I traveled to Paris, TX, to visit with the Crow's former pastor. Pastor James McCloud was their pastor when the accident happened, and even though he had moved away, they kept a close friendship to this day.

Pastor McCloud, also known as Mac, pastors Chisolm Trails Cowboy Church in Paris, TX. Mac said that he has known Tony for nine and half years. He could not remember where he was when he first heard of the accident, but as soon as he got the news, he left to go to Parkland Hospital in Dallas.

Mac remarked, "I was the pastor at First Baptist Church of Winnsboro at that time and Tony and Cheryl and their family were members and very close friends of ours. My wife was with me when we left to go to Dallas.

Mac admitted that before the accident, Tony

seemed a little reserved around him. He recalled the night that Mac's family had moved in to Winnsboro, and how they were staying in a house on the Spiva Ranch, out in the country.

Mac remembered, "During that time, Crow and Landon had brought us some firewood, and stacked it on the side porch. That is the first time that we had met them. He was very reserved, until we got to know each other. They invited us over for a quail feast, because Crow and Landon would go quail hunting all the time in West Texas. We connected right off the bat. Crow started telling me about his Aunt, and he kept describing this woman. He never said anything about where she lived. Finally, he told me that her name was Aunt Sally. Well, the more he described this lady, the more I began to realize that *I knew* who she was.

"Where does she live Crow?" Mac asked.

Crow spurted out, "Buffalo Gap, Texas.

"Are you talking about Shotgun Sally Rock?"

"You *know* my Aunt Sally?"

"Yeah, I met her at the end of her shotgun—one

time."

Mac told the story, "I went on to explain that I worked for an oil company at one time. Our company had poured some concrete in a creek bed on her ranch property. I had mud on my windshield, so I had scooped up water with a cup and was throwing it up on my windshield to get it off and Shotgun Sally made herself visible. She came out there to see who I was and when I looked up, she had her shotgun pointed directly in my face.

Truth is, Sally is not his biological Aunt, but they became such close friends, that she became Aunt Sally to the Crow family. Sally had a mountain out there called, Sally's Rock and Mac's company used to work out there on it.

The fact that Mac knew Tony's Aunt Sally opened up a door up for their friendship to blossom. Crow started being himself more and more, and because he is such a cut up, Mac said that they developed an immediate kinship. Both of them love to hunt and fish, so that made their friendship all the more special.

Mac grew serious, "The most important words I had ever heard a man say is when I walked into that hospital room, and Crow's eyes were all bandaged. Of course, there was hope at that point that he might be able to see again. There was no indication that the ophthalmic nerve had been severed as of yet.

That is when Tony said, "Mac, I'm just worried about Landon. I am going to be okay no matter what happens to me, whatever the outcome, it does not matter. All that matters is Landon."

Mac reflected, "I spent a considerable amount of time with Crow following that day. I never once saw or heard a hint of bitterness towards his son, though we knew that Landon struggled. The impact that following Sunday morning service at church was enormous and we had a special time of prayer asking God to spare his sight and allow him to be able to see. We had some doctors in our membership, and one of them came to me after the service and said, 'It's probably not a real big concern, as they can do so much these days.'"

Mac thought about it much differently, knowing

the accident involved Tony's eyes. The reason for the big concern was because of the amount of time that had passed since the accident. Mac spoke with his wife and suggested that he would give Tony one of his eyes if need be. Even though Mac was clueless on how all of that would actually work, and admitted in his own words that he was "stupider than a stump" when it came to science, he decided to consult with the doctor at the hospital about it. He found out then that an eye donation would be of no consequence at the time because Tony's ophthalmic nerve had been severed.

"Crow is as much a brother to me as my blood brothers, and I just wanted him to see again, Mac stressed. After the accident, and as a pastor, I tell people often, when they are going through something that I have not experienced, I do not know how they feel, or do I pretend to. I have seen a lot of accidents and deaths, and I have discovered that it is not so important to try and say the right thing, but to be as natural as you possibly can. Crow and I both are big cut ups, and that has not changed at all. He is going to give me a hard time about whatever he can, and I do not give him one bit of slack. One thing that impresses me about Crow when he is listening to a baseball game, especially the New York Yankees, I can call him and ask him what he is doing, and he will say, 'I'm *watching* the game.' He still talks like that . . . I mean, he says he is *watching,* when he is listening.'"

After the accident, when Tony just needed something to do, he would go with Pastor Mac on visits to see other people in the church who needed help, or encouragement. Tony called Mac one time and let him know that if he ever needed him to go along on a visit, that he would be glad to do that. Things weren't always that way, especially right after he got home from the hospital. He did go through some depression. Mac alluded to it when he said, "After all, the humiliation of a man who is a man's man having to depend on someone else and go to what I call the 'blind school' in the Northeast, was particularly hard on any family, but especially on Crow. Before he went up Northeast to the blind school, he had to learn to walk with his blind man cane across a street and to let other people know he was there. The first time out, someone ran over the tip of his cane, while he was standing there in broad daylight. That was a frightening thing, but he soon overcame his fears and does extremely well today."

Mac laughed out loud and began to tell me some funny stories about Tony. "One time, I drove up on the Crow Farm to find Tony doing something absolutely mind boggling. Mind you, Tony has no light sensory or innate way of sensing direction. He can feel the sun on his face and that is his only indication of what direction he is going. Can you imagine my surprise when I saw a blind man out mowing his yard? After seeing Tony do that, I had him driving my truck. At the time, his daughter Candace pulled up and anxiously got out of her car and scorned, 'What are you all doing, you're crazy!'"

Mac continued, I drove up on another day to find that Crow was artificially inseminating his cattle. I hollered, "Crow, you still do that?"

He answered, 'Well, Mac, think about it! You

don't have to see inside the cows to artificially inseminate them.'"

Mac recalled another incident, "One time we were together driving down Highway 37 and in just a short while I noticed that Crow had gotten very quiet, and after looking at him, I could see a faraway look on his face. I asked, 'What's up Crow?'"

He said, "Mac, where are you going?"

"We're going to Tyler."

"Then you need to turn around, you missed the turn off." Tony warned.

Mac laughed, "Now here is a guy who can't see, can't tell light or dark and he is telling me that I missed the turn to Tyler, TX. Guess what? He was right!"

Mac said that he remarked, "There is nothing like having a blind man showing you where to go. This truly *is* the blind leading the blind!"

Once they got back to that road, Tony was telling Mac everything that was coming before they ever arrived there. Mac enjoyed telling me the next story. "If you are not familiar with Cator Hill, it is the highest point in Wood County. One time we were coming back from the hospital, and there was a man driving a chicken feed truck. He was looking for the Noble Farm so that he could deliver the feed. This guy was lost, and stopped to tell me where he was going.

I said, "Now I could tell you where the place is . . . but they have quite a few houses up there."

Crow had his cane folded up chimed in, "Which house you going to?"

Now Crow had turned and looked at the man, and that man looked at him and listened. Mind you, he kept looking at Crow, then me, and then his look became even more puzzled, because Crow was describing to him in detail exactly where to go.

That man leaned over to me and whispered, "Is he really blind?"

I answered, *"Blinder than a bat dude!."* That is when Crow just busted out laughing.

In closing Pastor Mac added, "One of the neatest things that I have seen come out of this whole ordeal is the commitment of a woman to her husband and the commitment of children to their father and mother, as well as Landon actually becoming a man through all of this. I realize that this could have wrecked Landon in a huge way, and I credit that they stayed true to the Lord and not blaming anyone. Crow has put this accident on himself. He says, 'If I would have done what I should have done, Landon would have seen me long before he had his finger on the trigger.' Crow was growing spiritually and in different ways as a man, and one day when we were talking I suggested that he share his testimony in church, and that day came to pass. I suggested that one day he might even start speaking, but he squawked at that. He never liked being in front of crowds. The grace in all of that is the fact that he does not have to look at them or see them."

As an outside observer, it was apparent that there was a kinship and friendship of total trust and respect for each other between Crow and Mac, and that it had nothing to do with Mac being a preacher. Mac laughs, "I still call him 'Crow bait or Old Crow,' and I'll tease him about things, and he will tease me right back."

Mac had a lot of good memories regarding Tony, and this one was no exception. Mac pondered, "Our church had a hay ride out on his place after we moved away. We brought a couple of horses there, as it was for a youth function. We brought three horses, and there was a big cook out, and hay ride and I was the designated driver who was going to drive Tony's tractor. He had a bucket on the front of it, and we were there parked right behind the house where his shop is located. It was a terrific place and all the kids were loading up on the hay ride. I was paying more attention to the kids on the back, more than I was the front of the tractor. I started taking off, and all the sudden I started hearing the sound of wood cracking. I had looked all over the place when I discovered that I had broken the main post off in two pieces with the bucket on the front of the tractor. Of course, everyone there was having a great time with this accident at my expense. Tony hollered out, 'Gateway McCloud—Man! I can't see anything, but I can drive that tractor through that big hole!' I told him that I would fix it when I returned. Before I got back with the youth, they already had it replaced and fixed, and of course, Tony was milking the situation for everything he could get out of it."

Tony hollered out again, "Oh Gateway McCloud drives through my fence, and tears it up and then takes off, and we have to fi x it!"

Mac laughed, "He will never let me forget that deal right there. Since then, any time I have used his trailer to haul my tractor or hay, he asked me, 'Are you going to be going through any gates? Should I call someone ahead of you and warn them?' There's no need to reiterate, but if you have not figured it out by now, Tony has a terrific sense of humor.'"

The following day after spending time with Tony out on the farm, I got to meet his best friend John Greer. I was glad to get to meet John, because he has known Tony from childhood, and they have always been close. I hoped to obtain a different perspective from him.

John walked inside, and it was difficult not to notice his presence. John sported a well-groomed, long beard, and has the stature of NFL player, even if he is not in that good of shape. For a big, burly guy, he is somewhat soft spoken and one can instantly see why Tony likes him. Tony considers John his very best friend. They have known each other since John was nine years old.

John started in, "I got to meet Tony when our family had moved back from Louisiana in 1964 and we lived on the north side of the town for one year before we moved to a red house on Beaver Street. Tony and his family lived on Post Oak. Our yards didn't connect, but there was a corner of the field in between us. Needless to say, it did not keep us distant enough from playing together. We became friends pretty quickly. We both played peewee baseball together. Through the years, before the accident, we were best friends. We did have some time due to life's responsibilities that we did not see each other much. Of course, it is a deal when you grow up together, and one of you doesn't get married, and the other does and their priorities change. It changes your relationship."

John was at home when Benny called him on Saturday to tell him about the accident. John admits that he honestly didn't think a whole lot about it. He chalked it up to hunting with someone else, and being peppered with shotgun residue. According to John, that is nothing uncommon and so he thought Tony had just gotten peppered, like he had seen so many times before. When John and Tony were kids, they would quail hunt often, but later in life, they had stopped hunting together. John never gave it much more thought until they arrived at Parkland Hospital and discovered a group of people there. The doctor came in and told all of us that Tony would be blind. John was able to go in and see Tony, along with Cheryl and the kids. He admits that it wasn't until the next week that Tony's accident began to affect him.

The accident with Tony caused some soul searching for John. He comprised, "I think what happened to Tony affected me more than when my own father died. Of course, dad had Alzheimer's and all of us expected things to deteriorate when he died in 1991. Tony's dad died in 2002, and the accident happened in 2003. At that time I was a welder. In fact, that is what I am today. Anyway, I would just be working on something, and when I dropped my hood to work, tears would just start running. Tony's accident had a sizeable impact on me, and it still does to this day. The accident makes me want to do things differently as far as be more safe in my approach at work. There are a lot of times now that I stop the people I am working with and tell them to think about the safety issues."

John said that he and Tony's relationship had not changed much since the accident except that they are much closer now. They talk a lot more on the phone then they did in prior days. Tony's family has always treated John like part of the family. He joins them for Christmas and holidays, because John considers the Crows his family.

One thing does irritate John in regard to Tony, and he could not withhold it. He shared, "Sometimes, if Tony has me weld something or do something and he wants to pay me, well . . . , we have a pretty big argument about that. Tony will say it does not matter what our relationship is, and that he would still need to pay me. Seriously, I feel like I need to be a responsible friend and do things like that, because I don't want money for it. I think others need to be more responsible for someone, especially when things like this happen. When he is around here a lot of people will get him by the arm, and help lead him, but I do not do that. He doesn't want to be babied, and I am not going to baby him. I can tell you this, Tony has always been there for me when I needed help, and I have always tried to be there for him."

John remembered, "Tony was so independent prior to the accident and thus he still surrounds himself with people who are independent. I think I let Tony do things that other people may not, because I know he is independent, and I want him to stay that way as much as possible. A lot of it is the fact that we're independent, bull headed, or whatever you want to call it, but Benny, Tony and I are all alike in that way and we get along well because of it."

Smiling, John added, "Tony and I have always had a great time doing things. His dad fished a lot, and we would frog gig, and we loved it. We did that a lot, and fished many times instead of doing our homework.

We found other things to occupy our time at night. We did not have a boat, so we would always go to the edge of the lake to fish or gig. What I admire the most about Tony is that he stops and thinks. I can remember right after the accident happened that he spoke at the church, and he said the biggest thing he had to do was to humble himself. After the accident, he lost a lot of his independence, and now he must ask others for help, and that is a humbling thing for a person like Tony."

Before we finished, John stated he had a few more things he would like to say, so he continued. "Now, Tony and I are both Yankee fans. When I was a kid in Louisiana, the first team I saw on television was the Yankees, and I have been a fan since then. That is Tony's favorite team too, so we hit it off and we still listen to a lot of Yankee games. I've been in Winnsboro, most of my life. This place used to be an oil town and major thoroughfare for travelers. It is mainly a peaceful town and people here genuinely care about each other. I do not think I have ever experienced another place like Winnsboro. The response that this town had to Tony's accident was unfathomable. There was such a large display of love and care after his accident and that itself, speaks volumes about our community. I would say our town is filled with God-fearing, hardworking people, and there is no other place that I would rather live."

After talking with John, I excused myself for a while as I wanted to focus on all the stories and experiences that Tony and his friends here in Winnsboro had so willingly shared with me. After meeting so many wonderful people I got a true sense as to what the heart of Winnsboro is all about. In a nutshell, Winnsboro represents a township where family, community, and faith are in the forefront. I myself grew up in a small community, but we were still very much distanced from one another. This is not true about Winnsboro. Lives here intermingle, and make deliberate choices to spur one another on in business and in family life. There is a tremendous support group here that has enabled the Crows to move on beyond the obstacles that they have encountered through the years. Tony has been a leading factor when it comes to exemplifying the importance of overcoming such obstacles. Part of that is inherited, as he is a member of the well-known Crow family. If you ask me, the other significant factor in this equation is the community of Winnsboro in itself. They may be small in comparison to other townships, but they are monumental in the things that count, and that attribute is genuine concern and love for one another. They prosper here because neighbors, friends and church family work together to ensure that everyone in this small town succeeds. The Crow's may be an entity of their own, but when you put all of Winnsboro together, they demonstrate the aspect of a very big family with one single goal in mind.

Of all the people I have met, the places I have seen here, and the stories that I have listened to, I would have to say that one single goal is to *love your neighbor as you love yourself.* Mark 12:31 (NIV).

CHAPTER EIGHT

The TXU "Family"

During my stay in Winnsboro, I had the privilege to visit the Luminate Power Plant where Tony worked until the day of his accident. As you enter the complex, there is a sign that says: "**19 years, 10,400,000 man hours worked, no lost time accident.**"

I had found it rather uncanny that a company that instills safety measures as stringent as this power plant would have an employee that would not take safety measures when they were off the work floor. Of course, most employees off the job have that mindset. Luminate's motto is *"Investing in our community, investing in Texas."* A safety conscious employee does not just happen overnight. It takes the investment of time and resources into an employee to make them responsible when it comes to safety matters.

As we drove onto the grounds of the power plant, after stopping at the security check in, Tony began to direct us on the road to the main office. Mind you, we have a blind guide telling us that the road is going to curve to the left at the top of a hill, and then the parking

lot will be on the right. I could not help but laugh out loud at how funny this whole scene was as I observed from the back seat. Tony's memory never fails him, and the fact that he led us right to where we needed to be in a matter of minutes, was astounding.

TXU Plant

After we walked in the door, people began to gather around us and talk to Tony. They never said their names, but he remembered every person by the actual sound of their voice. Tony literally remembered every person there, and you could see that it became a game with some of them.

For instance, one guy said, "Do you know who this is Tony?" He waited for Tony to figure it out, which only took a matter of seconds. "I couldn't forget you if I tried Mickey Woods! How are you doing?"

Tony caused quite a commotion, as news spread quickly that he was in the office, people started showing up to say hello to him. You could see the delight on their faces when they would greet him. I sat back and just absorbed it all. It was delightful to see that, after nine years, people from all over that plant stopped in to see Tony. Of course, Tony does go to the plant for a visit now and then, and that is perhaps why he has lifetime friends who would do anything for him. We found our places, and I was ushered to a back room to be able to interview a few of his co-workers from back in the day.

A Luminate North Region Safety Supervisor by the name of Ricky Foster was one of the first men that I met there at the plant. He has been working for Luminate now for thirty years. He has always been fond of Tony and insisted that Tony is a great guy, a good worker, and a man with strong work ethic. People at Luminate all like Tony very much mainly because he has a terrific attitude and he has always been family oriented.

Rick continued, "When I first hired on I was in the support side of company when it came to planning and scheduling. At that juncture, I did not have many interfaces with Tony, though I did know of him. When I moved into the safety division in 1991, that is when I started working closer with Tony. I never saw him as a fl ag waiver on the safety side of the job. That is not to negate that he wasn't safe. I think he was particularly safe, and I think he looked after others. I never pressed him on it when it came to talking to others about it."

Rick cannot remember where he was when he first

heard about the shooting accident. All that he can remember is how he was moved to pray for Tony and his family. He could not imagine what that would be like. It was the concern and uncertainty of not knowing how Tony was going to handle the ordeal that made Rick pray all the more.

Rick stated, "Our relationship now, is different. Tony and Pat Taylor and some people in corporate safety put a video together of the accident and talk about it, and it was kind of cool. They did an excellent job on producing that, and they distributed it here in the plant. I was somewhat of a visionary for what he does now. Through the years, I have had an opportunity to hear different people make presentations on safety. With that being said—when I heard Tony's message, I thought to myself 'Man— that is pretty good!' At the time, I was working closely with behavioral based safety. In essence, that means that you have a better opportunity in safety if everyone is engaged. It was here, at a Luminate based conference that we would share success stories to be an encouragement to employees. I had seen other people's presentations so I told Tony that his presentation was remarkably good, and I called him and asked him to consider just coming and doing a breakout session at the safety meeting, then a Power Pack session with a bigger room to accommodate more people at North East Texas Community College."

Following that, Rick went to Tony's house and they brainstormed, and Rick assured him that his message was powerful. Rick also asked Tony to come up with his dog and be the keynote speaker for a church Sunday school teachers meeting. He had already shared his testimony at his own church.

Rick added, "Well, he came and shared his story, and to this day, I still have people who ask me how Tony Crow is doing. We had a conference at the college, and I purposely stayed in those sessions with him. Everything that I envisioned happened there.

People would ask Tony questions like, "How do you get through stuff like this?" He would say, 'The Lord, my family . . . the support . . . etc . . .' I wanted to give him as much an opportunity that I possibly could for him to speak to people at conferences. So I assisted in that so as to get Tony some exposure. He did not have a lot of experience back then, so I would send letters out to prospective groups and tell them that his story would make a significant difference if they would have Tony come speak."

As a safety person, Rick asserted that Tony's message stresses the importance of safety both at work and off the job. Rick goes on to say, "Sometimes people look at safety with the attitude, 'Why are you bothering me with all that . . . just let me do my work!' I loved what Tony said in that first conference and I will never forget it. '*God closed my eyes, but he opened my eyes to a whole new world!*' You know a lot of people go through trials and circumstances and they don't always get it, but Tony gets it!"

Next, I met Rodney Whitter, the production Superintendent who has been working thirty-six years for the company. He had known Tony since they were both about five years old. Tony's dad recommended that Rodney try to get on at Luminate and shortly following, they hired him.

Rodney further added, "I was born in the same town Tony was born in, and our dads were devoted friends. They lived in a small house in town, and our parents played forty-two all the time. On the day of the accident, I believe that I was traveling somewhere. I was devastated when I got the call and heard what happened to Tony. We were talking with other friends here at work, and there was some hope that he might see again. It was extremely hard to find out that Landon had been involved too. Tony is like kinfolk to me. I cannot believe how Tony could deal with this whole crisis. We were afraid it would be something that would tear him down. Everyone was praying for him, and when we would call and talk to him, he always had that same good spirit that we have come to know and love. We raised around $5,000.00 to help support him in getting a seeing guide dog. Jeff Zimmerman was instrumental in starting that also. Everyone here has always thought a lot of Tony, and we all are very much like family. Tony is considered a personality these days, but he is still a very dear friend."

Rodney continued, "I use Tony as an example to other people here at Luminate. His faith and the way he held it together spiritually has been an enormous blessing to all of us. One time, when Tony was an equipment operator, he had just come back to work from having a serious bout with kidney stones. Even though he still had a problem with pain, he came back to work on a Sunday. Sunday's is the day that we usually conduct a test on the main turbine for the generator. This required Tony to hold the handle on the front standard of the turbine so that we could run the tests. It was essential that he hold the handle down, as it was a particularly delicate test. If he were to release it, the mistake would trip the entire board and consequently the entire unit would go down. I trusted that he could do the job, but I told him to let go of the handle, and we lost the unit. I was new at doing the test, but Tony knew what he was doing. I had my mind on Tony and his pain, and told him to let go. It was my fault, and as we could hear everything close and the safeties go off, we realized what we had just done. Well, we then turned and walked back to the control room."

Jack Rutledge, Supervisor in charge of Omissions at Luminate has known Tony for thirty-four years. Jack reminisced, "Tony has always been a loyal friend, a good work companion, and we would also do things together outside of the plant."

When Jack heard about the accident he was hoping it was a false rumor, as he was in shock. It was hard to imagine anything like this happening. The way that Tony has handled the accident, according to Jack is mostly a fitting testimony of his character. He insists that Tony has a positive attitude and that it is astounding to see the things that he has done without his eyesight.

Jack added, "During the time of the accident, I had just had surgery on my hip, after Tony had encouraged me to finally follow through with it, because he had surgery on his knee and had done so well with it. After the accident, you should have seen us together. I would guide him along while I was on crutches. That sure was some sight to see a man on crutches leading a blind man around!'"

During the time of this writing, Judy Narramore, the company HR Manager was a person that both the Crows wanted me to meet with, but at that time she was dealing with a health issue. However, I did receive some correspondence several months later, via Cheryl, and I thought it only appropriate to let you, the readers, hear what she had to say.

Judy wrote:

I had the privilege of knowing Tony as a friend and coworker for over 25 years. Prior to his accident, he was a leader at work, and his vibrant personality brightened up the room when he walked in.

After Tony's accident, I met with Tony and Cheryl at their home and discussed employee benefits. Prior to arriving, I struggled with the right words to say that would comfort Tony with his life-changing disability. After visiting Tony, for a few minutes, I was surprised that Tony's attitude towards his own adversity had lifted me up! I told Tony that I believed with his experience and amazing outlook, he could one day be a great motivational speaker sharing his story to help others.

A few months later, Tony accepted our offer to speak at an employee meeting and share his story from a safety leadership perspective. He delivered an amazing, inspirational message that touched the hearts and minds of everyone in the room. I knew from that moment that God had a plan for Tony Crow!

I am so honored to be acquainted with Tony and to see the impact he has had on the lives of so many people as he continues share his story.

Respectfully,

Judy Narramore

That day, as I walked through some of the plant and had seen the area where Tony used to work, known as the Control Room, I was privileged to meet many of Tony's former co-workers, and also met John Story, who has been working for Luminate for thirty-seven years. John is doing the very job that Tony used to do at Luminate. They both worked together in the same control room unit.

John smiled, "I have known Tony since 1977 when he was hired on to work here. Before the accident, Tony was very outgoing and highly talkative, once he got to know you. We worked together for several years. You see, once you are in the Control Room for twelve hours a day, day after a day you get to know someone pretty well. I was never a hunter or fisherman, but we got along well working here together. Tony is all about hunting and fishing etc., but when it came to people and politics we have a lot in common."

John recalled that he was at work when he received the call about Tony's accident. He said that Tony handled what happened to him as well as anybody could have. He continued, "You never heard anything negative come from him. He stayed strong for Landon's sake too. His personality is the same old Tony! He is 100% positive, and except for losing his sight, he is the same man he was before."

As I moved on, I met another worker who is also a very good friend of Tony's. "I have worked at

Luminate Power Plant for thirty five years, and I have known Tony for the same amount of time," Jeff Zimmerean proudly stated. Jeff recalls Tony as being serious on the job when he had to be and lots of fun at other times. According to Jeff, Tony is pretty much the same since the accident, and he has always been a practical joker.

Jeff was the one who came out to the plant to tell a lot of the guys about Tony's accident. It really caused him great sorrow, because he and Tony were, and still are very close friends. When Tony was in the hospital he requested one thing of Jeff.

Tony said, "Just don't forget me. I got a lot of visitors right now, but when this is all over with, people have a tendency to forget everything."

Needless to say, they have been pretty close ever since that time. Jeff takes Tony out to the sales barn to buy cattle and Tony, being who Tony is, raises his hand, even though he can't see what he is bidding on. He has gotten Jeff into lots of trouble with that, because Jeff is forced to buy those cattle.

Jeff added, "I was one who considered the idea

about getting Rudy. I got a calf donated, and we auctioned it off, and I think it was somewhere around $5,000.00 worth of funds that we raised for the cause."

Jeff implied that Tony is the type of guy that if a job needed to be done; well he was going to do it. One time, Tony went over to Jeff's house, and Jeff had his tractor in the bottom of the pasture. Jeff said, "I also had my truck and Tony was with me. I asked Tony, "Which one do you want to drive back to the house?"

Tony laughed at me and asked, "What do you mean? I am not driving anything. I can't SEE to drive!"

Jeff refuted, "Sure you can. There are no trees out here or anything that you can hit. Just listen for my voice and I will tell you if you need to turn left or right, and I will drive the tractor right beside you and guide you . . . so, come on!"

Tony followed Jeff's voice just as they planned and everything turned out perfect. Tony even parked the truck in Jeff's garage.

Now, as I am listening to Jeff tell this story, I immediately think of the scripture in Isaiah 30:21 "And your ears shall hear a word behind you, saying, "This is the way, walk in it," when you turn to the right or when you turn to the left." (ESV) English Standard Version.

I could imagine for Tony that learning how to trust Jeff by hearing his voice took an immeasurable amount of faith and courage. I can also imagine that since that time, nine years ago, Tony has learned how to tune in to that "Voice" when he has needed to do so. Perhaps, prior to the accident, he could not hear God's intimate commands to turn left or right, but now, as a blind man, he has learned to depend on God wholeheartedly. Maybe if you have never been faced with trials that have caused you to depend on God totally, you are much like Tony was back in the day. The Word says that those who cannot trust God are spiritually blinded, and realistically, all of us at one time or another has experienced this kind of blindness.

Two weeks, after Jeff guided Tony through the

pasture, Landon got his truck stuck down there on Tony's place. Tony was with him when it happened, and Landon said, "I am going to go get the tractor and pull us out."

After getting the truck out, Landon informed Tony, "Now Dad, I will go take the tractor up and then I'll come back and we can take the truck on up."

Tony jumped on the opportunity. "No, I can just drive beside you and you can tell me if I need to turn or not." He insisted.

Landon did just as his dad had told him to do, and successfully guided Tony telling him when he needed to turn. On their place, there was a lot more maneuvering that needed to be done to get the truck back from the pasture. Nevertheless, Tony made it back with the truck.

Jeff smiled, "I know it meant a lot to him because this all took place shortly after his accident. He has been challenged . . . and I try to challenge him on some things. It is unbelievable the things that he can do. Sometimes I go up to his farm and see him and Rudy working together and Tony does all this work on his farm, by himself."

One day, while visiting the Crow Farm, Tony told me about a time when he was at the plant and he was on unit three. It was at night around three or four o' clock in the morning when one of the junior equipment operators called and said they had a problem and asked Tony to come see if he could help. Tony willingly went there after hearing that a pit in the pump room had filled up with water. The supervisor at the time was not knowledgeable yet on what all needed to be done. He could not estimate where the problem was coming from.

Tony added, "I told him that there is only one thing that the problem could possibly be. Underneath this pit there is a valve that has been left open, and it is allowing the pit to be filled with water."

Tony assessed it and realized that there was more water there than you could pump out. There was not a pump large enough to remove the water.

The junior operator said, "I don't know where that valve is underneath that water. His supervisor said, "Well, I don't know where it is either."

Tony was next in line, and he has never been the type to let an obstacle get in his way. Tony discovered that one of his best friends that he had relieved from duty that day had left that valve open and forgot it, so the pit had filled up with water.

Being that they were down there on nights, and no one else was around Tony offered, "Hey guys, we've got to get this thing closed. Go over to the warehouse and get me a pair of throw away overalls."

When they got back, Tony stripped his clothes off and put on those paper overalls and some rubber boots and went down into that water that was four to five feet deep. Because of the location of the pit, Tony only had about three inches to raise his head up and get a breath of air before going back under the water. He would work on the valve just a little by closing it some, but then he would have to retreat to the top of the waterline to get a breath, only to return back to work on the big valve again. He did this numerous times, until he successfully got it closed.

When I came back up to the top of the water, I could hear them hollering, "Are you okay?!!" Tony recalled.

Tony answered, "'Yeah, I'm okay."

Tony concluded, "The water was very nasty, as only you could imagine. Actually, it was worse than nasty. It was just terrible. It had dirt and gunk in it, and after ten minutes, I came out of there, and those white coveralls were blackened with oil and other contaminants."

Tony climbed out and went straight to the maintenance shop to take a shower because he was covered in the silt from the pit.

After returning, they all agreed that what he did was not safe, nor did it comply with plant safety rules, so they would just keep the incident all to themselves.

Tony relays, "Think about it. I had no business doing that kind of stunt. It was dark, and with no safety line attached to me, I could have gotten hung up under there, and drowned."

Regardless of their word to keep the incident hushed, the truth eventually surfaced and Tony was found out. Tony said, "Again, there are certain things that happen out there that everyone always remembers, and it seems as though I am involved in a lot of them. For instance, one time I was out on the plant and the stack fell and missed me by fifty feet. Another time, we had a real bad fire on the boiler of unit two. I looked out the control room window and saw the fi re billowing out of there. One guy, who was my superintendent at the time said, 'You know, when you are on duty Crow, I sleep with one foot on the floor. It seems like you're snake bitten. It appears that every time that you are on duty, some kind of disaster happens.'"

After visiting with co-workers at the plant we all went inside to eat lunch together and the deep friendship between Tony and his former work friends was evident. They laughed about old times, and talked about his career now, and how none of them ever imagined that he would be traveling and speaking all over the United States. They were thrilled for him and that he had found his true calling in life.

Another heartwarming story that Tony shared with

me, displayed very well how his co-workers care about him and still do their best to be involved in his life.

A guy at work, Pat Taylor, sent an email to the New York Yankees and told them Tony always wore a New York Yankees hat and that he was shot and lost his eyesight. Pat told them that Tony was a huge Yankee fan and that he was hoping they would let him meet them sometime. He sent them the email to see what their response would be.

A month or so, someone in public relations with the New York Yankees called Pat and told him that they read Tony's story and they wanted to do something for him, so they asked where he lived. Pat told them and they said, "We are going to be in Arlington playing the Rangers in two weeks. If you can get Tony there, we will let him go out on the field and meet the New York Yankees."

At that time, Landon and Tony were coming back from a hunting trip in West Texas and Pat Taylor called him, as the guys at work were trying to surprise Tony with the news. They did not want him to know about it until he got there.

Tony relayed the story, "So, Pat called me and I answered the phone. He informed me that they had gotten some tickets to the Ranger and Yankees game and asked me, "Would you be interested in going?""

I answered, "Pat, I appreciate that, but I can get more out of the game by listening to it on the radio or television because of the crowd noise. So, just give my tickets to someone else out there at work."

Pat paused for a minute then replied, "Man . . . you're making this hard on me. I called you because I contacted the New York Yankees and they sent us tickets and said you can go out on the ball field to meet them."

Instantly I remarked, "I change my mind, I'll go!"

Tony continued, "Two weeks later Pat and Rodney brought their sons and came and got Cheryl and Landon and me to take us to the game. We had to get there several hours before the game, and they told us to meet them at the first gate. They were having batting practice when we arrived. The Vice President of the New York Yankees met us at the first gate and took us out on the ball field.

He then asked, "Tony, who do you want to meet?"

I answered, "*Joe Torre*, (The coach at that time in 2005) *Don Mattingly*, (the hitting instructor) and *Derek Jeter*.

After that they took Landon and Tony out on third base and the Vice President said, "Here comes someone you may know and it is not any one of the guys you had already told me that you wanted to meet."

Then *Mariano Rivera* came out to meet us on the field. One of the first things he said to me was, "Tony, I read your story."

Tony surprisingly continued, "Now one of the most amazing things to me was that a team that traveled as much as the New York Yankees, had time to read about my story. They knew about me and what had happened to me and Landon."

Mariano went on to say that he was sorry about what happened and was glad that I could come out for a special day to see them. He shook my hand and the guys signed baseballs for us. Mariano said to Tony, "My friends call me Mo, and I consider you one of my friends, so you can call me Mo."

After Mariano left another guy came out and Landon said, "You didn't ask for this one either dad."

"I was so taken back that these guys came out to meet me on their own. *Tino Martinez* came out to meet me and at that time he was the New York Yankee first baseman. He talked to me and signed the ball too. Following him came Don Mattingly, and then Joe Torre, who both singed the ball for me and talked to me for a while.

I could hear the batting practice going on, and then I heard Landon say, 'I don't have to tell you who is coming out now, do I?'"

I replied, "No son, I think I know."

Then I heard a man say, "Stick your hand out Mr. Crow. My name is Derek Jeter."

After shaking his hand, I said, "Derek . . . , my son would like you to do a favor for him."

"Whatever it is, I will certainly try to do it." He replied.

"He has a jersey and he would like you to sign the back of it." I explained.

Jeter said, "Well, if it has the right number on it, I'll sign it." Landon was wearing a New York Yankee *Derek Jeter* jersey and it was #2, Derek's number, so he agreed to sign it.

Derek asked, "You got a pen?"

In front of all those thousands of people who had shown up by then to watch the game, Derek signed Landon's jersey for him.

As we were walking off the field, Joe Torre

walked up to me, and Cheryl was up in the stands with her camera, so I asked if we could have a picture, and he was glad to do that.

Tony finished by saying, "After all that was done, I got to go back up into the stands and listen to the ball game, and it was a very special day. By the way, the Yankees won big that day, so that made it even a more of special day in all of our lives."

CHAPTER NINE

The Beginning of INJAM

Before I share some of the correspondence that Tony and Cheryl have received since the inception of INJAM, I think it is important that readers know what INJAM stands for and how the name came about.

Cheryl said, "Ten years ago when the accident happened, I wondered what we were going to do since Tony was blind, and we knew that he was not able to work anymore at the Power Plant. I wondered what he was going to do with his life. I was worried and praying many a night about our future—but when God shows up—He shows up big! I never dreamed we would be traveling all over the US non-stop. **INJAM** is now able to give Senior Scholarships and sponsor those to go on Missions all over the world. What an awesome God we serve!

Tony recalled that he was receiving request to come and share his story at local churches and also in the workplace. As requests grew, he and Cheryl both felt led to create a company that represented their efforts to educate people on the importance of safety and the detrimental effects on those who do not take preventative measures in the workplace or at home when it comes to making safety a way of life.

One day, Tony was out on the farm when he was trying to think of memorable name that might explain best what he was trying to tell people across America. The first response that Tony shares in this book after he realized how many people had come to the hospital to see him was, "*It's not just about me.*" As he pondered on that, he decided upon an acronym INJAM and therefore the company was formed. As an outsider, I read between the lines of the acronym and see how people are "in a jam" if they ignore the basic principles behind safety. I can understand why people responded with letters, emails, cards, and even newspapers and television stations were being enamored with the message of a blind man traveling and speaking about

safety.

• CHAMBER

(Continued from Page 1)

Wearing black sunglasses and helped to the auditorium stage by his wife Cheryl and his leader dog Rudy, Crow smiled as he faced the audience and began his talk this way:

"I can't see you out there. I'll never be able to see anything."

He then told the crowd of the support he received from the Winnsboro community following the accident that blinded him, and did so with occasional wry humor. He said he was taken to Parkland Hospital in Dallas.

"When I learned on Sunday that I was in Parkland Hospital in Dallas, I thought that wasn't too good — that famous man [President John F. Kennedy] that they brought there didn't make it out alive," he quipped.

He said he had a special nurse who always seemed to be at his bedside; he recognized her from the great-smelling perfume she was wearing.

"That Sunday (the day after the accident), she told me she'd never before seen so many people at the hospital," he recalled. "She said she was going out to the waiting room to count them. When she came back she said, 'I counted 72 people out there, asking about you.'

"The nurse then said, 'You must live in a special town. Here in Dallas, you'd never see that many people coming here on a Sunday to visit a friend.' "

Crow then said, "That's the kind of people who live in this community — people who will drive all the way to Dallas on a Sunday (to see a friend)."

He noted that financial support by the community enabled him to go to Detroit to be trained with, and given, his leader dog Rudy. He thanked the community for its support in helping him to return to a near-normal life, saying to the crowd, "Give Winnsboro a round of applause tonight."

And Crow concluded his talk with this advice:

"If something bad ever happens to you, take that lemon and make lemonade out of it. I look at myself and say, 'I took lemon and made lemonade out of it.' "

The audience then gave Tony Crow a standing ovation.

CHAMBER HONORS REYNOLDS, SPARKS BUT BLIND MAN'S TALK HIT OF BANQUET.

Throughout the years, Tony and Cheryl have received numerous letters filled with admiration, accolades and more. Tony wanted me to make sure, that you the readers, realize that he is not sharing these notes or letters with you in a manner of bragging or puffing himself up. I have been around Tony enough to know that he would agree with this scripture, *"Therefore, as it is written: "Let the one who boasts boast in the Lord."* 1 Corinthians 1:31 (NLT) New Living Translation.

Tony and Cheryl are adamant about crediting their success on what the Lord has done for them. As you read the following comments, notes and letters, you too will realize just how special Tony and Cheryl both are to so many people. As you read, keep in mind that business names have been omitted (### i.e.,) and names of those who sent letters have been changed for security purposes. The letters have also been left in an unedited format on purpose, so that you will understand that the people that are touched by Tony's story, are mainly hard working plant workers.

(*From a Major Steel Company*)

Dear Tony,

I just got home from the dinner where you spoke, and I just have a few things to say to you. I was sitting at the table next to yours during the dinner and your presentation which followed, and I wanted to/should have spoken with you in person but truthfully, I was crying and so emotional that I was afraid I would embarrass you by approaching you. My husband has worked at #### company for twenty-three years, and has been seriously hurt once. Along with that, he has experienced several near misses, not due to his or someone else's carelessness's, but just resulting from the nature of the work. It's loud. It's crazy dangerous and sometimes in spite of everyone's best efforts, crap happens. You are right about people paying attention at work, but not at home. I see it all of the time.

It seems like so many of us just bump through our lives without ever knowing our true purpose, or ever knowing without a doubt that we make a difference

218 | *Blinded, But Now I See*

every day. I struggle with this all of the time—just wondering if you really are a blip on anyone's radar. You, on the other hand, have to know that with every word you speak, every venue that you address, you save lives, as directly as if you were a doctor, the paramedic, the one doing the CPR. You are responsible for moms and dads coming home to their families, hugging their children, welcoming their grandchildren to the world. Because of you being willing to put yourself out there, every day, you make a difference. My heart is broken for your circumstances, and especially for your son, who will see the result of his innocent actions every time he looks at you for the rest of his life. I suppose that it's been much easier for you to acclimate to your new life than it has been for your son. I was so happy to hear that he is in the business of personal safety, because I know that every day, he saves lives also.

I don't for a minute believe you were just a "Regular Joe' bumping along without making much of a splash, until the terrible accident happened. I am sure you were always one of those guys who everyone want to be around and wants to be involved with. However... I believe the splash you made in your everyday world is nothing compared to the tsunami you create now with our inspiring story of courage, wisdom and your willingness to walk through your painful story over and over, until we get it. You are exactly where God has put you, for such a time as this, so that the ripples of your circumstances wash over people everywhere and lives are saved because of it.

I would compare you to the Christian Evangelist Joni Eareckson Tada, whom I just heard speak last month at a True Woman Conference in Indianapolis, Indiana. She spoke of being a 17 year old, sexually promiscuous teenager who bumped along in her life, not knowing how to change her circumstance, until she cried out to God one night, 'OH God, change my life, take away this physical obsession with sex that I have that makes me continue to sin against you!" Five days later she dove off a pier in Chesapeake Bay, and a rip tide caused her to hit the water at the exact time the water became very shallow. She broke her neck, and for the past forty-five years she has had no feeling below the neck. For seventeen years she was a normal person, living her life the way she chose to live it, but now because of circumstances beyond her control, for 45 years she has changed lives with her story. She said, "I never once asked God why He let this happen to me. I KNEW why He allowed this to happen. I asked for help, and he granted me request in a definitive way, in such a way that I would never be plagued by the carnal desires I had been trapped in."

Then she laughed and said, "Moral to the story, be careful what you ask for!"

Mr. Crow, you might not have asked God to use you in a powerful way nine years ago, but because of your circumstances that is exactly what is happening. I was honored to hear you speak and will never forget your story. Bless you, your wife, your children and the new granddaughter who will have a very, very special grandpa.

Sincerely,

Priscilla Warren

Cheryl and Tony,

I just wanted to follow up and tell you folks again how much I enjoyed Tony's speech. I had heard about him from some of the other oil company people who attended the annual Safety Leaders Workshop at the Woodlands early this year, but I was not present when he spoke at that event. Your message touched my heart and I could not stop the flow of tears. I sat there and thought about some of the poor off the job safety habits I have in my life, and how I can and will change my attitude toward off the job safety. Your message about safety was very thought provoking.

Being a Christian, I could tell that Tony is a very spiritual man with a spirit in the secular setting. That happens so rarely, and I don't think that I have experienced that in any other situation while at the major oil company that I work for. I felt so strongly that I could approach him and let him know that his 'Light is shining' though in such a spiritually dark world today. I went home and thought about his slogan, "It's Not Just About Me", and I felt the spirit impress on me that we can apply that to our spiritual lives.

The Gospel of Jesus Christ is not just for us, or about who we are, it is for everyone who is willing to listen. I also know that our choice to be in a relationship with Jesus Christ is not in vain. It has an impact on our children, grandchildren and our close friends. My grandmothers, my mother, and my father made a decision to and taught me about Him. I am so grateful for that because I don't know if I would be a in a close relationship with God, if they had not followed Christ. Tony, you are a man with "calling." You have God's anointing on your life, and that is something that not too many people ever experience. Your experience is one that can be communicated from a spiritual perspective, as well as secular. If you had not had a relationship with a God, then you could not have survived this situation with such a positive outcome and outlook. Our world is full of people with emotional wounds that have never been healed, because they do not know about the healing power of Jesus Christ. Perhaps God will allow you to share with others just how your relationship with Christ, was the key ingredient in dealing with your situation and healing the emotional wounds that are derivatives of the physical wounds. May God richly bless you both and continue to use you mightily in His kingdom. You will be in our prayers always. Don't hesitate to contact me if you ever need a prayer partner on any situation. I believe prayer is so vital to staying strong in the Lord in our world today.

Again, God bless you.

Lucy Oncoore

Staff Regulatory Specialist

Tony and Cheryl,

I know that today is a tough day for you, your family and friends, but I just wanted to share something with you. Recently, we, (#####) purchased your video and have been showing it to all of our employees (840 full-time and 200 part-time). We decided to provide lunch, and following the video we passed out safety glasses and ear plugs to all of our employees to take home. The impact your video is having on our workforce is enormous.

Our class today could not help but notice the date (10th anniversary of your accident) and we thought it would be an excellent time to show our appreciation for telling your story. As tragic as your account is, it is changing lives. There is no doubt that you have saved countless families the grief that you and your family have witnessed. Over the Christmas holidays my two sons and I went on our annual quail hunting trip. We have always worn our blaze orange, but this year we wore our safety glasses and ear plugs too. They have not had a chance to see your video, but they got the *Tony Crow* safety training on the way to our hunt.

Thanks again for sharing your story.

James Petty,

Safety Risk Manager

Hi Tony,

My name is Torrey Dennis. I had the honor in being from the group from Lancaster, when you spoke in New York. I have worked there for 11 years, and have sat through safety meetings all of those years. To be quite honest with you, I have never been so moved as I was yesterday with your story. Your passion is so deep, and so heartfelt, I would have a hard time believing that there wasn't another person in that room affected in the same way that I was. I just wanted to say, "thank you". Thank you for coming all the way to NY and speaking in front of our company. You are truly mesmerizing and inspiring.

I was hoping to meet you and your wife, and of course Rudy, (I am an avid dog lover), after your presentation, but unfortunately the agenda for the day did not allow for such time. So, instead I wanted to drop you a message. Thank you again.

Take Care and God bless!
Torrey Dennis

Dear Tony,

I want to thank you for your visit and presentation

in our cafeteria at our site with the (###) company, and your story, your delivery, your strength, your courage, your wonderful personality, and last but not least, your message.

A few days after your presentation, I overheard in passing from almost everyone saying we have to be more like Tony Crow. People are quoting you in discussions on how we need to be safer in our work habits. How we all need to know and follow the rules. The people quoting you were the workers. The company people were smart and just let the workers talk with each other as this was a normally scheduled safety meeting. The old tired, boring safety meeting had changed into something meaningful as we had a joyful meeting with some really good safety ideas to submit to the company's approval. Thank you for sharing and being the spark that lit a fi re under us. You showed us that we all need each other and every safe idea is an important one. Thank you most of all for reminding us that we were one big family and we owed it to each other to work, play and live safely.

Yes sir. You have the kind of grace in your words

and actions that the Bible talks about; one man to another, one worker to another and one friend to another. Simply, thank you for sharing your story.

That's one power-packed message in you, sir. You really touched us and made a difference. Your name will be used for years to come along with the messages. Your sense of delivery, of making us feel a part of your life as friends, and coworkers, reveals your ways is the best. The best way I have ever seen in my 58 years, and I have seen a few.

Sincerely,

Mark Royer

Tony,

I attended the 2011 Conference in Texas and I just wanted to say thank you for the story you shared with us. I will say it brought a tear to my eyes but it was a very powerful story! I appreciate people like you who go on and share their real life stories to help others in the safety aspect of life.

I wish you and your family the best and once again "Thank you!" Rudy was great too!

Irina Motinyo

Tony and Cheryl,

First, "Thank you" for taking the time to come to travel to our (####) company and share your story with us. I am a twenty-nine year old employee (welder) and avid whitetail deer hunter in NY. I have got to tell you both that I have been to a lot of *company* mandatory meetings with guest speakers, and none has even come close to moving me like TONY did today.

I also ride a Harley, so taking risks is just about what I place myself in every day . . . , but as you spoke, I'm not going to lie, I had tears forming in the corners of my eyes.

Your message came through loud and clear, sir. Again, "Thank you" so much.

Sincerely,

Jack

Tony,

You don't know me but I need to tell you that I am so glad that I got to hear your story today. It really hit home. I work at (###) company, and hearing you talk today was awesome . . . What you said, really hit a home run, and to sit there and not feel your pride in your family and friends . . . pardon the pun . . . a person would have to be blind not to take what you have been through and not use it 24/7. Thank you for making people think, and you know what? I promise you here and now I will never take what you said for granted Tony. Thank you from the bottom of my heart.

Robert Brown,

Assembler

Mr. Tony,

I just watched your story at http://www.injam1.com I thank you for your courage and your kindness in sharing your story. I know following a tragedy that it is very difficult to see the blessing or even the reason for the hurdle. I pray that your son has made peace with the event and I pray you continue to speak to the thousands that God brings to your video. I guarantee you that your words are never in vain and that you have saved many a person, a mother, a father, a son, a daughter . . . from not only injury, but also from possibly losing a life.

God never gives us anything more than we have the strength to deal with . . . and sir, I am grateful for your strength.

May your life be blessed, and may you see God's light within your darkness.

Sincerely,
Brenda Nuttmeir

Dear Cheryl and Tony,

Both Joni and I enjoyed meeting you and Tony, and of course Rudy, at the Risk Management Conference in CA recently. After learning of your amazing story, I am not sure who is more inspirational, you or Tony.

I can't even imagine what all you two have gone through, but I know it has been extremely difficult, physically and emotionally for Tony, and certainly emotionally for you, perhaps even more difficult in some ways than for Tony. However, you have somehow managed to not only deal with the issues at hand, but at the same time, demonstrate a zeal for life and a transparent love that will serve as an example for so many other couples, particularly those who have suffered a loss of their own.

I don't think I've ever seen a better example of mutual love and support in a marriage, nor two people obviously in love than you two. Your marriage was obviously a good one before the accident or else it wouldn't have lasted, but I know there must have been challenging times for both of you; however, you have managed to meet those challenges and still maintain a good outlook on life.

I want you and Tony to know that your strength has been an inspiration for Joni and me and has caused us to reevaluate how we view our lives. We lost our son in 2006 and have struggled to come to grips with this loss and the effects it has on our lives. Honestly, we've been feeling pretty sorry for ourselves ever since, but we've decided to change all of that.

While you and Tony's loss is different from ours, it is nonetheless, a major life-changing loss, and the two of you have set a standard for making the best of any situation that we're trying to copy. We figure if we can demonstrate just a fraction of the strength you two have shown, we'll be able to go on with our lives and find a level of happiness, something we have both pretty much given up on. You gave us the strength to try harder, and you set the example for us to follow. Thank you so much for your valiant struggle, for your struggle has helped us deal with our own struggle.

Warmest regards and God bless,
Roger and Joni Klugen

After reading that last letter, I was reminded of yet another passage that so explicitly describes the mission that Tony and Cheryl share with others. These letters were just a *few* of the chosen ones out of literal hundreds that they have received throughout the years. I know they would agree with me that when it comes to sharing the burdens of others, we are directed to do so. In scripture, Paul spoke very clearly as to how those who have struggled, are to help others who are struggling. *"Praise be to the God and Father of our Lord Jesus Christ, the Father of compassion and the God of all comfort, who comforts us in all our troubles, so that we can comfort those in any trouble with the comfort we ourselves receive from God."* (2 Corinthians 1: 3-4) NIV

Tony and Cheryl continue to be a bright light in the workplace arena, where most people are not allowed to share their faith. They simply comfort others by allowing them to see how God has brought them through storm after storm in their lives. They do not mention it as much as just being an example for others to emulate. Tony does not mention God very much at all during his presentation, but I think it is most interesting how people perceive his events, what they hear, and what they don't hear, yet are very much drawn to. The Crows know about the *"But if not for God . . ."* truth about how they have made it this far so successfully, and they never take that for granted.

INJAM is definitely an *in touch* company, as it effects every person who comes in contact with it. Of course the goal is to ensure that companies are raising the standard on safety, and making a difference not only at work, but making safety a part of their lifestyle, for their family's sake. I am sure Tony's mantra could be nothing less than, "Until all have heard!"

CHAPTER TEN

Looking Forward

During the writing of this story, Tony and Cheryl have been on a perpetual road trip with speaking engagements, which leaves extremely little time for family home life. I look back at this last year in their lives, and I marvel at how much they have accomplished as a husband and wife team. There have been so many lives changed by Tony's ability to communicate the importance of safety and family.

Since he is traveling so much, people ask Tony where his favorite place to go on vacation is, and he replies, "To go home." This is because his traveling itinerary keeps him and Cheryl away from home for a big part of the year. Home is one place where Tony can relax because he knows where everything is.

Unfortunately, shortly after I took on this project,

Rudy, Tony's' leader dog became seriously ill with cancer, and within just a matter of weeks he died. After several months have passed, the hole that he left behind has yet to be filled. It is not something that Tony can bring himself to talk about easily. In fact, we have only spoken once in a passing manner as I rendered my condolences. The team of three has once again become a team of two and certainly has left a lot more responsibility upon Cheryl. Time will tell if they ever will get another dog. There will be no way to replace Rudy in their hearts. Rudy was Tony's eyes. He was Tony's right hand man in many ways, and when you bond to an animal like Tony bonded with Rudy, these things take time, and no one is in a hurry.

Cheryl admits that Rudy held an extraordinarily special place in her heart. She remembered, "There were many times I would lay down in the floor and just hug and love Rudy and thank him for what he was doing for our family."

Unlike most pets, Rudy represented Tony's eyes. When Rudy came into the Crow home, he totally changed their lives. It allowed Cheryl to feel more confident that she could leave Tony by himself for a short time and go downtown, or go shopping for more than 30 minutes. She had the assurance in knowing that Rudy would care for Tony, and make sure he got back to the house if he had gone out on the farm to work. Rudy was in every means, a member of the family.

Cheryl recalled, "With his big, brown eyes, he seemed as if he could talk to me. When we got the news that Rudy was going to have to be put to sleep due to the cancer, it was devastating. When we actually got the final call that he would not be home after we got back from being on the road, our hearts were broken, and there were many tears shed."

Today, Tony tells his audiences that he lost his eyesight on Feb 15, 2003, and that he lost it again when Rudy died, as Rudy represented his eyes for the past eight years. Tony relayed, "There was a man in MI, when I went to leader dog training years ago to get Rudy, and I asked him, how many dogs have you owned?"

The man replied, "I have had five dogs through the years."

Astonished, Tony asked, "Five?"

The man continued, "Yes, I am sixty, and I was born blind"

Tony said in his mind he already knew that the time would come for him to be in need of another dog someday. Tony continued to ask, "What was like when you lost your first dog?"

The man responded, "Devastating."

"How long did it take you to come back and get your next dog after you lost that one?"

"Three years."

"That long?" Tony asked.

"It took me *that long* to get over it. Now, I live by myself, the only way that I have any independence is to get a dog. Now, when I need a dog, I just come back and get another dog immediately.

As Tony relayed that story to me, he finished by saying, there is no set time when I will get another dog. I know that eventually I will, but I can't go there right now. It is still too emotional for me.

I inquired, "Tony, how is the farm work getting done without Rudy by your side?'

"The farm work is getting done with the farm hand now. We do it together. David Estes is our farmhand, and he does an excellent job helping us out when I am home, and when we are gone on the road.

As the fall of 2012 came, they got word that they were going to be grandparents. Landon and Julie were expecting a baby girl. It was with immense joy that I received an email from Cheryl telling me the delightful news. This family has learned how to deal with adversity perhaps better than most of us and as you will see, that kind of testing continues to be placed before them so that they can shine and reflect the character of Christ.

I took the time to ask Cheryl and Tony what it was like to hear that they were going to have a grandbaby, and they both were transparent about the emotions that they were feeling.

Cheryl answered, "We were both majorly excited, but also knew that when the day would come of the birth of our grandbaby, that it would be filled with several different emotions. One, joy to be grandparents, but at the same time realizing it would be a day that we knew would be difficult, as Tony would never be able to actually see his precious grandbaby."

I realized as Cheryl shared such a profound reality, that they already knew their grandchild's birth would create a plethora of emotions, especially for Tony. However, they had no idea, that they may have almost lost the opportunity to ever see her, or Julie again.

In December of 2012, Julie was forced to deliver Macy, due to health complications. The baby weighed only *one-pound and ten ounces.*

Cheryl continued, "There will probably be many days of joy along with sadness for Tony not being able to see sweet baby Macy's face."

Tony pondered the idea a moment and said, "I was looking forward to being a grandparent, but I was in awe, as most parents are, when they realize that their children are having children. It was emotional, because I had made the comment one time during a presentation that I would never get to see the face of my grandchild."

During Christmas of 2012, the Crow family had made plans to be at home in Texas, as usual. Landon and Julie were coming in for the holiday, and hoping to spend up to five days there. Julie's grandparents live nearby in Hughes Spring, so part of their visit would be to see them. That is how they usually celebrate Christmas now, but as Cheryl would say, "*Macy wanted to give us a special Christmas present this year.*"

On December 5th, Cheryl and Tony had just arrived in Houston, Texas for a presentation the following day. They decided to go downtown and make sure of the location of the event, when they received a call from Landon. That was not out of the norm for Landon to call in the afternoon, as he often did that.

This time he said, "I have some news for you. Julie has been care-flighted to Wichita, Kansas as her blood pressure is dangerously high."

Landon first said if they cannot get her blood

pressure down, and that they would have to take the baby in 72 hours. Then he called back and said it had been changed to within 48 hours. Cheryl had already called the contact for the presentation in Houston and told them that Tony would have to reschedule the meetings, and that they were leaving for Kansas. On the way, Landon called again informing them that they would take the baby in the next 24 hours. Just before actually leaving Houston, because they waited for the work traffic hour to subside, Landon called again.

Landon and Julie Crow

Tony answered the phone and Landon said, "Congratulations, you're a granddaddy!"

The original plan was that Cheryl and Tony would be with Landon as Julie was giving birth to Macy, but actually, no one was with Landon and Julie when she gave birth. Her parents were about six hours away, and they were not able to be there until later that night.

Tony said he was very concerned during that time, as he knew Landon had a great deal of pressure on him due to Julie not doing well health-wise, and Macy being so tiny, making her a high risk baby. He knew that Landon could lose both his wife and his daughter and he wanted to be there for him.

They drove home, rested for about four hours, picked up Candace and left for Kansas. When they got there, they went into the NEO ICU wing where Macy was. At this time, Julie was still not doing very well, but there was hope she would recover. Macy was critical, but stable, so they got to see her, that is, everyone but Tony. He explained that it was very emotional for him, as no one could hold the baby, but everyone else could see Macy, except him. He had to rely on what others said about her, and deep down it was very difficult for Tony to come to grips with.

Cheryl said it was very difficult for Tony, as we could all see Macy in the incubator, but he had no visible access to her. One time, Landon guided Tony's hand in through the incubator, and Tony was able to touch her for the first time. It was a little scary, as there were so many tubes in and around her tiny body and Tony was afraid he might touch one or accidentally pull one out.

Around the beginning of February 2013, they drove up to visit Landon, Julie and Macy at the hospital. It was there, Landon asked his dad to take a seat, and he placed Macy on Tony's lap. Tony said the feeling was incredible, as he had not gotten to hold her before, like everyone else.

As soon as Landon put Macy on his lap, Tony thought to himself, "I FINALLY got to see her!"

Cheryl said 'It was an irreplaceable feeling to finally hold Macy and to get to see Tony hold her too, because he felt like he could *really* see her by feeling her arms, legs and face." She admits that she has never been around a baby that small, as Macy's arms looked as if they were like little twigs. There was no baby fat on them at all. When Landon sent pictures of Macy via a text message, it did not appear that Macy was that little. However, after actually seeing her, they realized how very minute she really was.

Cheryl proceeded to say, "God is always there to guide us through and even sometimes carry us through life's unexpected crisis. As soon as we received the first phone call from Landon, we contacted several friends, asking them to pray. Our friends then contacted the prayer chain at our church, and within a matter of minutes we had many people praying for baby Macy, Julie and Landon. The prayers of friends and family are what help support us through life crisis."

Tony agrees with Cheryl, but he said that when he walked into that ICU where Macy was, that there were fifteen other premature babies, so it helped him put their crisis into perspective. Unlike other isolated crises that the Crows have experienced, now they were sharing the same predicament with so many other families. It helped Tony to come to a better conclusion about the situation and to place his trust in God all the more.

The reality is that they have not been able to bond with Macy as of yet, since she is still hospitalized. They know that once she arrives home, they will be able to hold her and do that more aptly, at Landon and Julie's home. This causes them to be all the more excited for what the future brings when it comes to baby Macy.

Cheryl and Tony

Both the Crows could not be more proud of how Landon and Julie are handling the situation. Most expectant parents go to the hospital and are allowed to leave in a few days with their new baby. Since they live an hour and a half from the hospital, leaving baby Macy for the first time, in the full care of hospital staff was a bit overwhelming. In addition, Landon's career keeps him the busiest this time of year, so he has had to sacrifice his time in seeing Macy, and usually goes up to the hospital on Sunday afternoons and stays until Monday afternoon until he has to report back to work. Julie is a school teacher, and she had to take an extended leave of absence to care for Macy. She spends a few nights at the hospital every week, and all weekend, and will continue to do so, until Macy can come home. Since they have had to wait over three months to take their precious daughter home, they also look forward to the joyous day when Macy will be discharged from the hospital.

In the spring of 2013, Tony was a speaker for the International Hunter Safety Education Conference. While at that conference, he booked a trip of a lifetime—an African Safari in South Africa with Unico Safari's(www.unicohunting.co.za).

Remarkably, Tony was able to take down (7) animals with a laser on his rifle and with the assistance of Ronnie West guiding him to move the laser up, down, right, left and then to shoot. Below, you will see the extraordinary accomplishments that Tony made while on this trip. In fact, Tony has not only accomplished the feat of hunting (while blind), but made the all-time record book as he took a 40" Gemsbok.

"Gemsbok—Record book—40" horns

Tony & Ronnie"

Wildebeest—Tony and Ronnie

Tony with a record book White Blesbok

Kudo — Tony Springbok—Tony and Ronnie

Impala—Tony and Ronnie

Warthog—Tony

In the midst of speaking engagements, losing Rudy, celebrating the arrival of Macy, and trying to find some time at home, the Crows have also endured a flood at their house, a remodel on their kitchen, and Cheryl's parents moving far away. It seems like life is constantly changing and bringing them opportunities to grow spiritually stronger each day.

As INJAM has become a very successful company, Tony's popularity has also increased. He still is astounded at how people react to an old country boy like himself. I credit that to Tony being able to articulate in a manner that many people wish they had the guts to. For instance, Tony is pretty black and white. With that being said, he just says what he is thinking, and calls the shots just as they are. He doesn't know the first thing about pretense or façade. If there is anything that family members and friends can relay about Tony, it is the fact that he is *true to himself*, and perhaps that does leave behind a bit of envy each time he stands up to speak in front of a crowd of people.

On a personal note, seeing this couple in action has inspired me to do more workplace ministry. It is easy as a Christian to play it safe, never mention God, never give Him credit, and hide under the radar so others do not know that you adhere to Godly principles in your life. As I have been penning this life story, a bit of my own life story has been affected. I see things a bit clearer than I did before, and I understand the passion that the Crows have to share the Gospel by simply allowing God's presence to permeate their lives in every aspect.

They don't have the need to talk about it all the

time. When they travel, when Tony speaks, when they meet strangers and when they are with family, their focus is God-centered.

After hearing this story, I wonder how many of us keep every aspect of our lives God-centered. What we are like in the workplace and what we are like at home when it comes to safety should be *seamless* in our lives. Tony Crow and his family have proved to us that God can be an intricate part of our work and play, and we can take him from church into the world. In other words, our relationship with Him should remain seamless.

In closing, I know Tony would agree with me, that leaving home to go hunting without safety gear would be like committing a grandiose act of foolishness. It is just as foolish to leave church without God. We need both safety nets to navigate this world successfully. The message of safety, though never spoken out loud in a conference, goes way deeper than an orange shirt and pair of safety glasses. It is the unique fabric entwined in our lives when we realize our vulnerable weaknesses and come to our end of independence, while becoming dependent upon God. It is remembering that there is "joy" in the journey. That is the "joy" that Tony has first handedly experienced, and it is the same joy that men and women throughout this nation witness as Tony speaks at his conferences. It is also the same joy that I spent four days with in Texas.

Scripture tells us in Nehemiah 8:10, "The joy of the Lord is my strength." (NIV) New International Version.

Never in all of my years of traveling, writing and speaking have I encountered such as a contagious joy as the one that Tony Crow wears now, and parenthetically, he wears it very well! I am convinced that Tony would have it no other way, and if you have the opportunity to hear him speak, you most certainly would agree.

Moving forward, Tony and Cheryl continue to book heavily as his safety presentations are on high demand. They are learning a sense of balance and trying very hard to adhere to what life is showing them through the journey. It has been a great ride so far, and they continue to credit each other and the Lord for their great success.

Today, Tony Crow and his wife Cheryl run a nonprofit called INJAM, or It's Not Just About Me. For more information, visit www.injam1.com or email Tony at: tony@injam1.com

Client's Tony Crow has spoken for:

Aera Energy

Albermarle

American Greetings

Ameren

Andarko

APAC

Arch Coal

Bandera Electric Co-Op

Big Country Electric Co-Op

BP

Brandon Shores Power Plant

BST National Safety Conference

Boeing

Cargill

Cascade Natural Gas

Chevron

Clayton Homes

Commanche Nuclear Power Plant

Con-Edison

Conoco Phillips

Constellation Brands

Constellation Energy

D. A. Collins

Denbury Resources

Domtar, DSM, Dupont

Energy Solutions

Entergy

Excel Energy

ExxonMobil

GM

Greif

Hargroves Engineers

Hawkeye Community College

HighMoutain Exploration and Production

Holy Oil Corp.

Intermountain Gas

IPL

ITT

Jacobs

John Deere

Kimberly Clark

Lancaster Development

LandAir

Lower Colorado River Authority(LCRA)

Longview Fibre

Luminant Energy

Lyondell Basell

Motiva

Mullet Crushed Stone

National Safety Conference

National VPPPA Conference

New Jersey Utility & Transportation

Nooter Construction

NRG

Nucor Steel

Oncor Electric Delivery-Transmission & Distribution

ONEOK

PCS Nitrogen

Peoples Telephone Co-Op

Pioneer Natural Resources

Plateau Telecom

Portland General Electric

REC Silicon

Regeneron

Rifenburg Construction

Sandoz

Safe Harbor Water Power Corp.

Shell

Sherwin Williams

US Steel

Valero

Wagner Power Plant

Wood County Electric Co-Op

XTO Energy

<u>Keynote Speaker Clients:</u>

Alaska BBS Conference

Arch Coal Eastern & Regional Safety Meeting

Carolina Star Conference

Constellation Energy National Meeting

Dival Safety Summit,

International Hunter's Education,

John Deere Joint Union Safety Conference,

Luminant Energy Behavior Safety Conference

Mississippi Manufacturers Conference

Missouri Mine & Health Safety Conference

MSHA Refreshed Training Seminar

NMRCGA Conference

Oregon Telecommunications Assoc. Conference

Osha Oil & Gas Conference

PBR Conference

PDRMA Safety Conference

Piedmont Natural Gas Safety Summit

Pulp & Paper Conference-Canada

Region I, IV, & VI-VPPPA Conferences

S T A F Conference

South Central Mine, Health, and Safety Conference

Telecom Annual Risk Management Conference

Texas Electric Co-Op's Loss Control-Conference
(TEC)

Texas Electric Power Conference

Texas National Safety Conference

Texas Statewide Telephone Plantmen's Conference,
(TSTCI)

WEI Safety Conference

Western Pulp & Paper Conference

Made in the USA
San Bernardino, CA
19 March 2017